Fifteen-Minute Retreats

TO SLOW DOWN YOUR WORLD

JOSEPH J. JUKNIALIS

World Library Publications
Franklin Park, Illinois

Author: Joseph J. Juknialis
Editor: Michael E. Novak
Copy Editor: Marcia T. Lucey
Typesetting and Design: Chris Broquet
Editorial Director: Mary Beth Kunde-Anderson
Production Manager: Deb Johnston

WLP 017110
ISBN 978-1-58459-377-5

Contents

Introduction

People tend to think of retreats as lasting several days or even longer, devoted to prayer and meditation, and located in some secluded place. It can be hard to schedule time to get away for something like that. But a retreat can be much shorter and much closer, as long as it fulfills its function of renewal. If your life is like those of many people in North America at the beginning of the twenty-first century, you are juggling multiple competing demands on your time and attention. Family life has to balance with professional responsibilities, and time is at a premium. And while you know that prayer is important in so many ways, at times it can seem like just one more thing that you don't ever get to on the "to do" list. *Fifteen-Minute Retreats to Slow Down Your World* is a collection of brief getaways designed to fit into your busy life and help you rearrange your priorities. Sometimes you need a breather, or just a reason to stop and gain a new perspective on what's going on in your world right now. Here are Bible-based meditations that can enable you to allow God to speak in the midst of your hectic day, and maybe even slow it down to a more human pace. You don't have to find a hermitage, and you don't need to set aside a week. Just open this book when you feel frazzled, take a deep breath, exhale, and start to slow down.

Each reflection in this volume begins with a passage from the Bible, moves to a brief meditation that addresses some aspect of the Bible reading, and concludes with some questions for reflection. While you can take as much or as little time as you like, five minutes for each part—fifteen minutes for the whole exercise—may be just what you need to recharge your batteries. On the next page is a suggested process for setting these reflections into a context of prayer.

How do you choose which one might be helpful today? The title of each "retreat" tells something of what it is about, so you could scan the table of contents for a likely candidate. You could go through the book in order, one meditation every day for a month (there are thirty). Or you can consult the index at the back, which lists the scripture citations and key words associated with each reflection. In that way you may be able to find what you need for your situation today. Or just open the book to a random page and dive in. God speaks to us in any number of ways.

Tips

FOR MAKING A FIFTEEN-MINUTE RETREAT

Ideally, a retreat takes place in a quiet space away from the hustle and bustle of your life. But if you are in the middle of a busy day, it may not be possible for you to follow all the suggestions listed here. Nevertheless, they are offered to help you make the most of the meditations in this book. Feel free to adapt these ideas to your own situation.

Retreat

It is good to take these retreats in the context of prayer. If you can, find a room or at least a quiet corner where you will not be interrupted during your retreat. Lighting a candle may help set the tone. Start with a simple prayer to place yourself in God's presence, perhaps something like this:

> Loving God,
> your presence fills all creation.
> Open my ears to your words,
> that I may grow in appreciation of your love
> and become a minister of your gracious presence
> in everything that I do.
>
> This I ask in Jesus' name,
> who is Lord for ever and ever.
>
> Amen.

Read

Slowly read the scripture passage at the beginning of the retreat that you have selected. Take time to allow the words to reverberate in your heart. Is there a word, a phrase, an image that strikes you at this time? What does this reading say to you here, now, today? After some time for reflection, read the passage again. What is the good news in this word of God?

Reflect

After thus allowing the scripture to speak to you, begin reading the reflection. Take notes if you like. Have a conversation with the author. Do you agree with what he has to say about the reading? Do you have a different insight into the sacred text? Is there something new that the author gives you to think about? Allow the printed meditation to inspire your further reflection about the scripture passage and how it relates to your life.

Respond

A couple of questions are given at the end of each retreat. After your dialog with the reflection, read these questions and respond to them. Some are invitations to further reflection. Some are invitations to do something in your life in response to the reading. Sit with the questions for a while and see where they lead you. Do they spark additional questions? Do they give you ideas for something you can do when you are finished with this reflection? How will your day, or your life, be different because of this time you have spent in God's presence?

Begin to bring your retreat to a conclusion with a prayer of thanksgiving to God for this time that you have been able to spend in reflection and prayer, or perhaps with some prayers of intercession for the needs of others. Finally, conclude with the Lord's Prayer.

Return

Having concluded your fifteen-minute retreat, find ways to carry with you the sense of God's presence that this respite has afforded you.

Fifteen-Minute Retreats

TO SLOW DOWN YOUR WORLD

GOD WORKS
IN THE DARKNESS OF OUR LIVES

[Jesus said to his disciples]: "Be watchful! Be alert! You do not know when the time will come. It is like a man traveling abroad. He leaves home and places his servants in charge, each with his work, and orders the gatekeeper to be on the watch. Watch, therefore; you do not know when the lord of the house is coming, whether in the evening, or at midnight, or at cockcrow, or in the morning. May he not come suddenly and find you sleeping. What I say to you, I say to all: 'Watch!' "

Mark 13:33–37

*T*hese days I live in what had been for well over a hundred years a convent for the School Sisters of Notre Dame who once taught in the parish's grade school. Like every old house it has a bagful of curious noises that escape and scurry around at night. Creaks and clatters and clicks ricochet about in this nighttime house that never seem to be heard in the daytime house. And because all of us who live here are adults, we say it's just the noises of an old house bedding down for a sleep—until one of us is home alone at night. Then, when the others return, we rush to tell them how Mother Caroline was up and about again, that German-born nun who brought the religious community to Milwaukee and settled them here at the parish. The dark does crazy things to our imaginations and makes us act and think like kids again.

In some ways the dark is like death. We never quite get used to either of them no matter how many times our paths cross. At best we grudgingly learn how to live with darkness, yet always and cautiously keeping it at bay. The dark has a way about it, flaunting itself with fearsome noises and mysterious unknowns. And when not only our bodies but also our very lives find themselves in the dark, when we don't know how best to deal with disciplining our children, or where to direct the rest of our lives, or how to manage a relationship, such darkness can seem unbearable. Then the dark is too much with us.

Such spirit-darkness, the Gospel says, is also when God comes into our lives. It is the time when the lord of the house returns—during evening time or at midnight or at cockcrow when the night begins to call out to the yet unborn day, or even at early dawn, that in-between time when darkness has not yet fully surrendered its grasp and new light still moves gingerly. Such darknesses are times for the arrival of God.

Maybe that is part of why we feel so unsettled by the darkness, because we're never quite sure what mysterious unknowns God might raise up at those times, though sometimes I wonder if even God knows. After all, the prophet Isaiah says that God is the potter and we are the clay. And anyone who has ever created out of clay or with paint or music or words or spices and foods or fabric or whatever one creates with knows quite well that when one starts the process, one never arrives where one has planned. So also, it would seem, with the divine potter. If God works and creates mostly in the dark, it may be because God, too, is in the dark about where it will all end.

On the other hand, perhaps we fear that all of those creaks and clatters and clicks are the sounds of our lives being rearranged for us without our having any say in the matter. Who knows then if we'll be able to live with ourselves when the new light dawns? Nevertheless, that is when God comes and does what God does—in the dark of our lives and not in the noontime light when everything is so obvious.

That may also be why each of us in our own crazy way tries to befriend the dark's noises. We say they're the sounds of an old house or the day cooling down or the furnace kicking in—or we say it's Mother Caroline. One way or another we find a way to live with the God of our darkness. For who knows what God may yet do with the damp clay of our lives?

13

The darkness can be a quieting time.
Set aside a time to be still and quiet.
Imagine what it would be like to befriend
your current darkness.

What do you fear from the darkness in
your life?

MYSTERIOUS GROWTH

[Jesus said to the crowds]: "This is how it is with the kingdom of God; it is as if a man were to scatter seed on the land and would sleep and rise night and day and the seed would sprout and grow, he knows not how. Of its own accord the land yields fruit, first the blade, then the ear, then the full grain in the ear. And when the grain is ripe, he wields the sickle at once, for the harvest has come."

He said, "To what shall we compare the kingdom of God, or what parable can we use for it? It is like a mustard seed that, when it is sown in the ground, is the smallest of all the seeds on the earth. But once it is sown, it springs up and becomes the largest of plants and puts forth large branches, so that the birds of the sky can dwell in its shade."

Mark 4:26–32

There isn't a preacher around who won't tell you stories of failed and tarnished preaching miraculously turned to gold. Everyone who has ever preached has walked back to the chair thinking that if what they just preached was not the worst homily ever, then it was certainly the second worst—only to be told by someone on the way out with tears in their eyes that the homily had touched them more than anything had in a long time. And the preacher thinks, "I have no idea how that could have happened."

The opposite, of course, is true as well. When preachers think they've been most eloquent is also when grocery lists have been written, vacations planned, and marital disputes mentally replayed. All of which says something about who is really in charge.

In her book *The Artist's Way* Julia Cameron builds a case for synchronicity. She insists that if anyone wants to do something good in life, then life will serve up the means to make it happen if we are open to it. Life will and does bring goodness to those who seek it. She unpacks an entire shopping bag of examples to support her thesis. It is, of course, just what Jesus has said all along. "Whatever you ask the Father in my name he [will] give you" (John 15:16).

The point is that much of life, maybe even most of it, happens without our contribution, and at times in spite of what we contribute. Children grow into remarkable adults out of violent and abusive homes. Congress somehow untangles itself from hopeless gridlock. People grow holy in a church that at times seems to oppress rather than nurture. Goodness and love sprout from lava fields of selfishness. Obnoxious sinners become charismatic saints. And like the gardens we plant, we have no idea how it all takes place.

If the kingdom of God happens through us and not so much by us, why make any effort at all? Don't we then slip and slide into indifference? We can never be quite sure how to balance individual responsibility with that twinkle in God's eye that seems to smile at our presumptions and then goes on to do whatever God does.

We really don't have an answer for that most necessary balance. Though we believe that the reign of God comes about through us, it also happens mostly without our realizing it. So while we go on building cities, God builds the community. We advance medicine, God heals. We raise families, God shapes and forms human spirits. We tinker with the Church, God brings people to faith. We dream dreams, God is the sandman sowing the dream.

Nor is it the mighty oak that is the most likely material out of which the kingdom is built. Rather, Mark's Gospel seems to suggest that God's most workable material is what one might call scrub growth—like the mustard seed that grows into a large but hardly majestic shrub. Not to say that God would not work through the more powerful nation or the more illustrious church or the more notable individual—just that it's no more likely that God would do so.

In many instances it is the children who bring parents back to an active faith life. It is the Church in developing Africa and in the barrios of South America that seems most alive. It is the wounded healers, people who themselves have struggled with pain and sorrow and sin, who are often the most effective healers of others. It is the poor who embarrass the rest of us by their trust and simple faith.

In the midst of such paradoxes the Lord Jesus tells tales of wisdom from another gene pool, tales of a divine inclination to draw life into all that it can be and to do so unfailingly. In fact, life is really happening beneath the fragile crust of our own bumbling struggles and not in what we fancy to be so important. There, Jesus points out, universes are evolving and being exchanged. There, new worlds are coming into being beyond what we can even imagine. And the grace of it all is that we need not know how or where, because God is the garden in which we are the harvest.

How do you balance personal responsibility for a just and caring world with the belief that it is God who ushers in the kingdom and not we?

CHOOSING WHO WE WANT TO BE

When it was evening, after sunset, they brought to [Jesus] all who were ill or possessed by demons. The whole town was gathered at the door. He cured many who were sick with various diseases, and he drove out many demons, not permitting them to speak because they knew him.

Rising very early before dawn, he left and went off to a deserted place, where he prayed. Simon and those who were with him pursued him and on finding him said, "Everyone is looking for you." He told them, "Let us go on to the nearby villages that I may preach there also. For this purpose have I come." So he went into their synagogues, preaching and driving out demons throughout the whole of Galilee.

Mark 1:32–39

For the past sixteen years I've watched and listened to Julie grow up. She lives in a family with four older brothers whom she sometimes despises but usually adores. And if imitation is the highest form of flattery, for most of those sixteen years she has wanted to be what those brothers wanted to be. So her dreams have wended their way through truck driver, to professional soccer player, to astronaut, with side trips into computer whiz-dom, marine biology, and writing. Her most recent vocational dream is environmental law, but don't ask anyone in Julie's family where that came from because no one knows—not even Julie, except that that is what she wants to do with her life, she says. And she declares it with such conviction that I suspect she just might find her way there. She keeps insisting that someone has to care about the larger world, and she wants to be that sort of person.

In one way or another, I suppose, we all become the kind of person we want to be—more the inside than the outside, probably, but to some degree the outside as well. Certainly our outsides are limited by the gene pool in which we swim—no matter how much we may want to play basketball in the NBA, it probably won't happen if we were born to parents who never grew taller than five-foot-six. Nor will it happen, at least at this point in history, if we happen to be born female rather than male. So for good or for ill, our outsides do bump into some inbred and cultural limitations on our becoming who we want to be.

For the most part, however, our insides seem to grow to reflect the dreams and desires we choose to befriend. In other words, if you or I honestly long to be someone who is patient or generous or trusting, it will come about sooner or later, as long as that longing is more than some fanciful wish and as long as we're willing to pay the price of sacrificing our own way or our own fortune or our own security.

Of course the shadow side is also true. If what we long for is to be rich or famous or glamorous, we may well become greedy or self-centered or superficial. But in the end, we do always become the sort of person we want to become. So if Julie does not become an environmental lawyer, she will at least become someone who cares for creation.

The real question, then, is what sort of person do any of us long to become, and how do we give that decision all the attention it deserves?

We might start by acknowledging that there is something to be said for the times we spend alone. They may be the times thrust upon us, as they were for Job when he wrestled with the devils of darkness who dragged him through the barren and bitter nighttime. There Job confronted his life and his God. Or they may be the times we choose for ourselves, as Jesus did when he got up early in the morning in order to go off and sort out what the real purpose of his life should be. The silence of the desert refused to allow him to be distracted by the clamor of life.

We all can find such times. Sue loves to iron clothes. In the process, she says, she also irons out her life, all its wrinkles and creases. She says she can stand neither her clothes nor her life when they're all rumpled. John runs every day. He hasn't missed a day in five years. But it's also when he paces out the rhythms of his life. More than one frazzled mother has locked herself in the bathroom for twenty minutes of solitude and quasi-peace. Sometimes deserts look like bathrooms. Even teenagers know the need, so they crank up some tunes, stretch out on their beds, and listen beyond the music to the melodies playing in their lives.

I suspect there is a lot going on in those quiet spaces. That's where kids get raised and loves get sorted and businesses are merged and decisions unraveled and re-raveled. But somehow at those times, we also make some decisions about who and what we want to become in this life—at any age. That's when goodness has a chance to surface and values are affirmed and commitments are remade for the umpteenth time and faith sprouts forth. And then it becomes prayer, out of the silence and the stillness and the darkness.

Can you recall a time when you chose to become something specific? Was it your outsides or your insides that you were considering?

At this point in your life, what do you want to become?

TRUSTING ENOUGH TO SAY YES

In the sixth month, the angel Gabriel was sent from God to a town of Galilee called Nazareth, to a virgin betrothed to a man named Joseph, of the house of David, and the virgin's name was Mary. And coming to her, he said, "Hail, favored one! The Lord is with you." But she was greatly troubled at what was said and pondered what sort of greeting this might be. Then the angel said to her, "Do not be afraid, Mary, for you have found favor with God. Behold, you will conceive in your womb and bear a son, and you shall name him Jesus. He will be great and will be called Son of the Most High, and the Lord God will give him the throne of David his father, and he will rule over the house of Jacob forever, and of his kingdom there will be no end." But Mary said to the angel, "How can this be, since I have no relations with a man?" And the angel said to her in reply, "The holy Spirit will come upon you, and the power of the Most High will overshadow you. Therefore the child to be born will be called holy, the Son of God. And behold, Elizabeth, your relative, has also conceived a son in her old age, and this is the sixth month for her who was called barren; for nothing will be impossible for God." Mary said, "Behold, I am the handmaid of the Lord. May it be done to me according to your word." Then the angel departed from her.

Luke 1:26–38

*W*e all seem to have been conceived with a peculiar genetic characteristic known as the why-chromosome. Somewhere around the age of three or four we begin to ask why, and subsequently only the words that follow seem to change.

Toddlers want to know the ultimate why. Why do birds fly? Why does grass grow? Why do people get sick? After a brief, if any, respite, adolescents re-enter the world of why. Why can't I go out? Why can't I have the car? Why can't I have the friends I want? Adulthood once more exchanges one set of whys for another. Why is there evil in the world? Why must children die? Why does God not stop war? Once the switch for that why-chromosome is flipped, it seems to stay on for a lifetime.

We live in the ambiguity of why. As often as anyone attempts to suggest an answer, it never seems to satisfy—or perhaps it's more the case that the only answers that satisfy are the ones we discover for ourselves. The toddler is not content to be told that birds fly because they have wings, nor is the teenager content with the explanation that the need for rest is the reason why he or she must stay home. The adult cannot accept the reality that much of the evil in the world is of our own making as human beings, and that perhaps God is powerless to intervene and undo our doings. We seem bent on discovering the answers for ourselves. So we live with ambiguity, at times insisting on our desire to have life served up our way, as did Adam and Eve, and at other times willing to say yes to what comes our way, as did Mary.

Yet sometimes we are not sure which is which. Is the prospect of a divorce simply the result of one's own yearning to be freed of the struggle of making a marriage work, or is divorce or separation the conclusion that will make everyone healthier and more whole? Is one's sexual orientation nature or nurture, to be accepted or to be condemned? Is rejected love a tragedy or a painful door that opens to richer life? Is the decision not to have a child born of selfishness or of selfless care for the family as it presently is?

It is seldom clear when to say yes and when to say no. Which alternative is of God and which is of our own clouded longing is often subject to wondering, particularly when we realize that none of us ever decides from the purest of motives.

So we live with ambiguity, like Mary. In the end, I suppose we, too, must resist the temptation to insist upon clarity and understanding. Life seldom is served up with such garnish. Most often we find ourselves simply coming to the point of saying yes without having any of our whys sufficiently answered. Sometimes living in ambiguity is the most Godly thing we can do.

Recall some of the times of ambiguity
to which you offered up a hesitant
or reluctant yes. What came of those
responses?

Given the option, would you choose to
live a life without ambiguity? What might
be gained? What might be lost?

LISTEN FOR GOD'S CALL

Samuel was sleeping in the temple of the Lord where the ark of God was. The Lord called to Samuel, who answered, "Here I am." He ran to Eli and said, "Here I am. You called me." "I did not call you," Eli said. "Go back to sleep." So he went back to sleep. Again the Lord called Samuel, who rose and went to Eli. "Here I am," he said. "You called me." But he answered, "I did not call you, my son. Go back to sleep."

At that time Samuel was not familiar with the Lord, because the Lord had not revealed anything to him as yet. The Lord called Samuel again, for the third time. Getting up and going to Eli, he said, "Here I am. You called me." Then Eli understood that the Lord was calling the youth. So he said to Samuel, "Go to sleep, and if you are called, reply, 'Speak, Lord, for your servant is listening.'" When Samuel went to sleep in his place, the Lord came and revealed his presence, calling out as before, "Samuel, Samuel!" Samuel answered, "Speak, for your servant is listening."

1 Samuel 3:3b–10

*T*here are times when we find ourselves haunted by the question that we manage to keep at bay during the busy days of our lives: What do we want from life? Or to put it another way, perhaps more anxiously: What am I supposed to do with the rest of my life?

If I might borrow an image from the poet Annie Dillard, each morning is like going to a cottage for summer vacation. When you open the screen and unlock the door, at that moment you have all the vacation ahead of you that you're ever going to have. So what are we to do with this slice of future life that we find ourselves juggling like a hot roll from the oven? Do we just follow the path of least resistance and fall into a lifetime of choices made by others? Is there a way to choose wisely? Is there a call from God that we need to listen for? How do we know which instincts to follow? How do we do the sorting and know where the Godliness of any call lies?

Whether you are young or old, there is a wonderful tale about sorting such a call and what to look for as you open the screen and unlock the door to the rest of your life. The story is that of Samuel and his call to be a prophet to the people of Israel. As it was, Samuel hadn't planned any such thing. The story begins during the nighttime, when Samuel is asleep in the temple where he is apprenticed to the priest Eli. Through the darkness belonging to the night and to his own dreams, he thinks he hears a voice calling his name, so he goes to Eli, thinking it was the priest who called. Three times such dream-confusion rouses young Samuel and twice Eli tells the youth to go back to sleep, that he had not called him. At the third such rousing, Eli suggests to Samuel that it might be the Lord who calls, though one also wonders whether it might not also be Eli's frustrated need to get a decent night's sleep that he passes off on God.

At any rate, Samuel returns to his quarters and to his dreams, and as it turns out the Lord was indeed calling the youth. After all his wandering in the dark, Samuel finally answers, "Speak, for your servant is listening" (1 Samuel 3:10). That is also when Samuel begins to understand what his life is to be about.

Samuel's story is a useful guide for sorting out what God calls us to do or be, whether to religious service or to another vocation. First of all, the call comes in the dark, sometimes that of the night but also the darkness of our living and uncertainty. If you find yourself in the dark, then, don't run from it. Dare to live there.

Second, Samuel needs the silence of the nighttime to hear the call. So if you need to know where God is calling you, whatever your age or stage in life, make sure you have some silence in your life, some quiet time and some daydreaming.

Third, we need to be willing to go where the call leads. Honestly saying "Speak, Lord, I'm listening" can be scary but also exciting.

Fourth, don't be afraid you'll miss the call. Trust that God keeps calling, sometimes because, as with Samuel, we don't recognize the summons as coming from God, but also at times because we're too busy or we don't want to go where it leads. Trust God's persistence.

Finally, find a mentor to help you do the sorting, as Eli did for Samuel. Mentors or spiritual directors notice what we miss. Share your journey with someone who knows how to listen and who knows the ways God works.

At this point in your life, do you need new direction? Try the "Samuel steps" outlined above.

Who in your life serves as a mentor? Who has wisdom to offer?

WHOSE TIMELINE DO YOU FOLLOW?

[T]here was a wedding in Cana in Galilee, and the mother of Jesus was there. Jesus and his disciples were also invited to the wedding. When the wine ran short, the mother of Jesus said to him, "They have no wine." [And] Jesus said to her, "Woman, how does your concern affect me? My hour has not yet come." His mother said to the servers, "Do whatever he tells you." Now there were six stone water jars there for Jewish ceremonial washings, each holding twenty to thirty gallons. Jesus told them, "Fill the jars with water." So they filled them to the brim. Then he told them, "Draw some out now and take it to the headwaiter." So they took it. And when the headwaiter tasted the water that had become wine, without knowing where it came from (although the servers who had drawn the water knew), the headwaiter called the bridegroom and said to him, "Everyone serves good wine first, and then when people have drunk freely, an inferior one; but you have kept the good wine until now." Jesus did this as the beginning of his signs in Cana in Galilee and so revealed his glory, and his disciples began to believe in him.

John 2:1–11

If it's true that each of us is not the center of the universe or even the still point of our swirling galaxy, then why do we expect God's timeline and everyone else's to coincide with ours? We put forth much energy trying to rearrange life to coincide with our own desires, yet we do it all rather ineffectively. Too often our failing efforts become a source of mounting tension.

All around us are numerous timelines that tangle themselves into one huge snarl of throbbing life. Beyond our own timeline looms our spouse's and our children's and our parents' (whatever their age or ours). Friends have expectations of us as well, and society, too, and of course that place we call work. They all seek to impose timelines on us of one sort or another, calendars and agendas and responses set to their whims.

And then, of course, there is God's timeline, which never seems to be in sync with ours. Either God seems to lag behind our hopes and plans—resulting in a snowstorm of petitionary prayer—or God seems far ahead of what we are willing to agree to, resulting in anger and frustration and even what theologians call sin, that is, choosing not to do the good that would be in our best interest. Usually we just drag our feet into wherever it is we're going to end up anyway.

The cacophony of such timelines out of harmony is all around us. Talk to graduates who come to the end of their education. Society's time "to go out and earn a living" clashes with the twenty-one-year-old's "I don't know what to do with my life." Or consider the couple longing for a child yet never conceiving; or conversely the couple who unexpectedly find themselves to be with child and so also with their farsighted plans in disarray. Or those desperate to fall in love though no one's path crosses their own. Or premature death when lives spin out of control. Or the empty nest that comes too soon and before one is ready to relinquish the longing to feel needed; or just as readily the adult child who has decided to return to the nest. It is rare that timelines converge or agree, and hardly ever ours with God's.

So why should Jesus be any different? He finds himself at a wedding, presumably a celebration of friends and neighbors. He's there to enjoy that gathering, to play and not work, and least of all for his life to break open. His mother says, "They have no wine." He says, "It's not my concern. My hour has not yet come." She says to the servers, "Do whatever he tells you." The clashing of timelines.

Do whatever he tells you! Mary said it to the servers, but she might just as well have been saying it to her son. Do whatever God tells you! It's at that moment, if we say yes, that a new creation happens, that a new banquet is spread before us, that a new marriage binds us with life. It's at that moment that we are led into some new way of being, and in John's Gospel it's at that gathering that the Word-made-flesh begins to sing a new song that everyone begins to hear with new ears.

Do what God tells you, but how do we know what God is really telling? Perhaps we know when all of life insists on saying one particular thing to us, or when all of life is saying what we would rather not hear. Or when most of life is saying it. Or a part of life that will not allow us to back away is saying it. That's one way of knowing. In the end either we say yes or our lives go so flat that all we have left with which to toast life is water, no wine, and then the celebration that we call life comes to an end. So most of the time and after much squirming we find ourselves saying yes.

Are we ever ready? Sometimes, but not very often . . . and mostly not at all.

Which parts of your life are going as you planned? Which aspects are following some other timeline? Which might be helpful to readjust?

Name the three best things that ever happened to you. Whose timeline shaped them?

LONGING FOR A BETTER WORLD

When the days were completed for their purification according to the law of Moses, [Mary and Joseph] took [Jesus] up to Jerusalem to present him to the Lord, just as it is written in the law of the Lord, "Every male that opens the womb shall be consecrated to the Lord," and to offer the sacrifice of "a pair of turtledoves or two young pigeons," in accordance with the dictate in the law of the Lord.

Now there was a man in Jerusalem whose name was Simeon. This man was righteous and devout, awaiting the consolation of Israel, and the holy Spirit was upon him. It had been revealed to him by the holy Spirit that he should not see death before he had seen the Messiah of the Lord. He came in the Spirit into the temple; and when the parents brought in the child Jesus to perform the custom of the law in regard to him, he took him into his arms and blessed God, saying:

> "Now, Master, you may let your servant go
> in peace, according to your word,
> for my eyes have seen your salvation,
> which you prepared in sight of all the peoples,
> a light for revelation to the Gentiles,
> and glory for your people Israel."

The child's father and mother were amazed at what was said about him; and Simeon blessed them and said to Mary his mother, "Behold, this child is destined for the fall and rise of many in Israel, and to be a sign that will be contradicted (and you yourself a sword will pierce) so that the thoughts of many hearts may be revealed." There was also a prophetess, Anna, the daughter of Phanuel, of the tribe of Asher. She was advanced in years, having lived seven years with her husband after her marriage, and then as a widow until she was eighty-four. She never left the temple, but worshiped night and day with fasting and prayer. And coming forward at that very time, she gave thanks to God and spoke about the child to all who were awaiting the redemption of Jerusalem.

Luke 2:22–38

35

*I*t was mid-December and the red-and-green combustion of Christmas was everywhere. So when our arms brushed it seemed no more than another tumble of the crowd making its way through the mall. Then I heard my name called out and turned to look back. "It's me, Paul. Remember me? From Christ King?" I did, easily, though the last time I had seen him he was in grade school and I was an associate pastor there. He'd grown up now, taller than I, married, and a father, too, he quickly and proudly proclaimed. Then Paul did what every new father has always done since the invention of the camera. He pulled out his wallet and began flipping through the pictures of his daughter—one as a newborn, another at three months, another at six months, and yet another at somewhere-in-between months.

"I've been thinking about you," he said to me, "wondering about where you are and how I might get in touch with you. I'd like to have her baptized and was wondering if you would be able to." Paul grinned. He was pleased with himself, I could tell, for wanting to do what a good parent does.

"Oh, that's a marvelous thing," I told Paul. "Do you belong to a parish anywhere yet?" I asked him.

"No, not yet," he went on to explain. "My wife isn't Catholic and she goes to another church, but she said it would be all right if our daughter was baptized Catholic. I'd like her to get a Catholic education. You know, Catholic grade school and all of that."

The mall swirled about us in a frenzy to make sure that Christmas would happen, yet there stood Paul in a very different Christmas field of dreams, somewhere between the memories of his own childhood, with what had been sown in him, and the early stirrings of his daughter's new life, with what that life might harvest in her. Like Simeon and like Anna, who both came to the temple longing after longing in search of an ancient promise to be made flesh, so Paul and all parents come to each day with a silent and unspoken hope. And they too stand there before that temple, believing not only that their child's life can be filled with holiness and peace, but also that something in that child can be the very revelation of the God who is in our midst.

I doubt that most parents think about it in those terms. I'm sure they don't. But they do look upon their own love made flesh and find themselves believing that maybe this child could be more than they themselves ever were. This yearning is at the center of creating family, a mysterious urging of the human heart that will not die from one generation to the next. In Simeon-and-Anna-like fashion, it is the soul-deep belief that life can be more than it is—not simply comfort and ease but goodness and grace and wisdom so pure that it can be touched and known and cherished no matter how many swords may pierce our lives, and maybe even because of the swords.

Family is family, it seems to me, because we struggle to nurture in one another what so often no one else will. So we clothe ourselves with mercy and kindness and meekness and patience. We choose to be willing to bear with one another, even when we would prefer not to. We forgive grievances and strive to put on the sort of love that holds us all together. Could any of us be family without that?

A part of me suggests that it happens all by instinct, much as it seemed to happen to Paul. But then another part of me believes just as surely that that instinct is none other than the very grace of God upon each of us, refusing to abandon a soul-deep longing that this crippled world of ours be made whole.

What events have sparked for you the belief that life can and will be more than it is?

Among the people whom you know as family, what longing burns eternal?

GOD FEEDS US

Jesus went across the Sea of Galilee [of Tiberias]. A large crowd followed him, because they saw the signs he was performing on the sick. Jesus went up on the mountain, and there he sat down with his disciples. The Jewish feast of Passover was near. When Jesus raised his eyes and saw that a large crowd was coming to him, he said to Philip, "Where can we buy enough food for them to eat?" He said this to test him, because he himself knew what he was going to do. Philip answered him, "Two hundred days' wages worth of food would not be enough for each of them to have a little [bit]." One of his disciples, Andrew, the brother of Simon Peter, said to him, "There is a boy here who has five barley loaves and two fish; but what good are these for so many?" Jesus said, "Have the people recline." Now there was a great deal of grass in that place. So the men reclined, about five thousand in number. Then Jesus took the loaves, gave thanks, and distributed them to those who were reclining, and also as much of the fish as they wanted. When they had had their fill, he said to his disciples, "Gather the fragments left over, so that nothing will be wasted." So they collected them, and filled twelve wicker baskets with fragments from the five barley loaves that had been more than they could eat. When the people saw the sign he had done, they said, "This is truly the Prophet, the one who is to come into the world." Since Jesus knew that they were going to come and carry him off to make him king, he withdrew again to the mountain alone.

John 6:1–15

*A*ge, even just a little bit, brings perspective. I remember once hearing my grandfather lament how the young people of my parents' generation wanted all the good things of life without working for them, and how they wanted them all as they were beginning life. No one wanted to wait, he complained.

Years later I remember my parents bemoaning the fact that my generation wanted to begin adulthood with all that their own generation had spent a lifetime acquiring. If we had it all as an appetizer, then what would be left for the main course?

Last week I was with some friends at a social gathering. The conversation turned to a critique of the emerging generation. With a frown of disapproval someone there observed that Generation X had it all now, and what would they have left to experience in the second half of life? Surely life would leave them disappointed.

I smiled to myself and thought how life does tend to repeat itself. We are indeed the sons and daughters of our parents.

Such angst seems shortsighted, for it presumes that for each life there are only a limited number of experiences, and once they are used up, life as it waits to be lived is over. Then all that remains is the dying. If that is true, then God's imagination is indeed limited.

Such thinking presupposes that all of life and growth and becoming takes place in the external forum, in the world around us. Once we attain the pinnacle of acquisition, then we and life have arrived, converged, and now reign. None of that, however, recognizes the internal growth of the human person—living with humility and meekness and patience as Saint Paul at times reminds us to do, bearing with one another lovingly and seeking a unity that binds us to one another, or any of the other dimensions of being human to which Jesus continually calls us.

Paradoxically, our overflowing toy box just might turn out to be a grace, part of God's "sneaky" plan to bring us to where God wants us. Perhaps the sooner we are disillusioned of the notion that our toys can bring us happiness, the sooner we will begin to journey into the richer aspects of life. A midlife crisis could become the entree into an unimagined transformation of our spirit as we rethink what truly matters and where the journey really leads.

The fact is that God's basket of bread and fish holds much more than we can even imagine. It is true that God nourishes us with life—with home, whether cottage or castle; with clothing, both plain and fashionable; with food, whether simple fare or banquet; with travel to the bus stop and beyond. But God's nourishment is much more.

By all the twists and turns of life, by its tragedies and its gifts, God brings us as well to generosity and trust, to wonder and gratitude, to justice and love and service of others. Such is the food we really feed on. Such is the banquet at which we really gather, and of that there is more than we could ever dream, more full baskets left over than we could ever count.

The rush to acquire life's possessions has a limited future; in the basket of bread and fish that God distributes it is only a morsel. Of course it never satisfies for very long. There is so much more. Not to worry, however. It is God who does the feeding because after all, as Jesus tried to show Philip in our passage from John's Gospel, God knows what God intends to do all along.

How has what nourishes you changed in the last five years? Ten years? Twenty years? How has it sustained you for more challenging experiences?

As you anticipate midlife or reflect upon your experience of midlife, what feelings about your life come to the fore?

FINDING YOUR SOUL

[Jesus said:] "Amen, amen, I say to you, whoever does not enter a sheepfold through the gate but climbs over elsewhere is a thief and a robber. But whoever enters through the gate is the shepherd of the sheep. The gatekeeper opens it for him, and the sheep hear his voice, as he calls his own sheep by name and leads them out. When he has driven out all his own, he walks ahead of them, and the sheep follow him, because they recognize his voice. But they will not follow a stranger; they will run away from him, because they do not recognize the voice of strangers." Although Jesus used this figure of speech, [the Pharisees] did not realize what he was trying to tell them.

So Jesus said again, "Amen, amen, I say to you, I am the gate for the sheep. All who came [before me] are thieves and robbers, but the sheep did not listen to them. I am the gate. Whoever enters through me will be saved, and will come in and go out and find pasture. A thief comes only to steal and slaughter and destroy; I came so that they might have life and have it more abundantly."

John 10:1–10

A friend brews beer for a hobby. Not a lot; two cases every three or four months. So this Easter Sunday when he announced it was time to uncap the latest effort as one more way to embrace life, all of us gathered around. He poured the first bottle out into four glasses; we toasted his generosity as well as the new brew and then tasted his labors. It was flat, like resurrection called back into the tomb. There was no carbonation.

It had the smell of beer, the familiar whiff of hops. It had a golden mellow color. The fermentation was there. Everything was perfect except that it was flat. It didn't have any soul.

This trait that we call "soul" is a curious thing that we're not always sure how to find or even what it might be. Richness or depth perhaps, or sometimes meaning. Maybe energy, or gusto. Panache is another word people use, whatever that may be. Nevertheless, whatever soul is, without it not only beer goes flat but everything else as well.

When our lives go flat and lose their soul, many folks end up tossing that part of their life away. When a job is no longer exciting, some go job hunting. When a marriage grows stale, some seek another way of life. And then there is "midlife"—a time that seems to be cluttered with life that's lost its soul.

Obviously we wouldn't choose that for ourselves. On the contrary, we put forth much effort to preserve the soul of our lives, even when we are not quite sure what we are trying to preserve. I know some would say there's a difference between one's soul and whether or not the beer has gone flat, and of course they're right. But I also wonder if what we mean when we say that our life seems to have gone flat or lost its soul and what we mean when we worry about losing our soul aren't the same thing, or at least close to it.

Every once in a while you and I get lost in our search for what we sense is missing, and our search for soul (only we don't call it that) loses its focus. We say we need to put some life back into our lives or we need more air in our balloon. Maybe it's when someone tells us to get a life. Or maybe it's when we end up feeling sorry for ourselves and so we pull down the shades not only on our living room windows but also on our deepest insides, on our hopes and dreams, and we sit in a darkness that is heavier and more fearful than any nighttime walk through a cemetery. Whenever that is, that's when we realize that if our life has lost its soul, so too has our very being. It feels like life without purpose or meaning or maybe even God. At that point we desperately long for someone to show us how to find our way back to the light. Enter Jesus, the shepherd.

In truth, whenever you and I follow the way of that shepherd, our lives seem richer. They seem to have soul— when we care for others more than for ourselves, when we forgive (even though grudgingly) or are generous or peaceable or faithful. And whenever you and I do not live in such a way, that's when everything goes flat, even the beer.

So we say Jesus is our shepherd, because when we feel lost nothing or no one else seems better able to show us how to be found.

Has your life ever been drained of soul? What was it like? What brought the soul back to your life?

What's the role of God in your need for life to have soul?

I MAKE ALL THINGS NEW

[I, John,] saw a new heaven and a new earth. The former heaven and the former earth had passed away, and the sea was no more. I also saw the holy city, a new Jerusalem, coming down out of heaven from God, prepared as a bride adorned for her husband. I heard a loud voice from the throne saying, "Behold, God's dwelling is with the human race. He will dwell with them and they will be his people and God himself will always be with them [as their God]. He will wipe every tear from their eyes, and there shall be no more death or mourning, wailing or pain, [for] the old order has passed away."

The one who sat on the throne said, "Behold, I make all things new."

Revelation 21:1–5

*T*here seems to be a longing deep inside us, a yearning to be made new. Though it swells and ebbs, it never really ever goes away. It just waits for another time to show its face.

A while ago a brand of cleaning products launched a new toilet brush, one that has the liquid cleanser and disinfectant stored inside the handle. Television became its midwife, promoting it as a new generation of toilet bowl cleaner. The ad concluded with a series of "housewife" testimonials, the final one of which attested, "It has changed my life!" This was nothing but another appeal to our hidden longing that our lives be made new.

Consider the abundance of television makeover programs: one for back yards and front yards, for the outside of one's home or the inside, for one's basement or one's attic, for one's style of dress or one's style of living or for one's physical appearance, even to the point of a surgical makeover—the "extreme makeover." Each of us in some way longs to be made new, sometimes vicariously and sometimes directly.

The music charts a while back highlighted a release by the Indigo Girls titled "Closer to Fine." It's about searching and not finding and still searching, everywhere and anywhere, to discover a way of becoming who we are meant to be, and so finding a way of being re-made, of being made new.

In spite of all our efforts that for the most part seldom bring about what we seek, the song points out, it is when we cease the seeking that we grow closer to being fine. It is as if another power at work in our lives can bring us closer to that for which we long, if only we let it do so.

It is one of the paradoxes of life: the more we seek ourselves, the more we lose ourselves; and the more we are willing to lose ourselves, the more we find ourselves. This is, of course, only another way of speaking about love.

It seems simple enough. If your life is in chaos or disarray, if you find yourself unsettled and discombobulated, then forget about your own life and begin to focus on the lives of others. Lo, your own life will then begin to settle into place, and you will grow closer to fine. Love works this way, if indeed love does any work at all. It is love that makes us new. It is the ultimate makeover, because God is love.

On the rocky island of Patmos where Saint John lived in exile, he had a vision. There he heard a loud voice from the throne saying that God "will wipe every tear from their eyes, and there shall be no more death or mourning, wailing or pain, [for] the old order has passed away . . . Behold, I make all things new" (Revelation 21:4, 5). This is how God who is love works.

Weapons will never create a new Iraq; only compassion will, and justice, and heartfelt care for the Iraqi people. Even the military leadership of the coalition understands that. It is why so much effort is given over to schools and infrastructure and food.

Punishment and the inhumane conditions of prison life will never remake the soul of one who is incarcerated; only hope for a future will, and education, and nurturing the human spirit.

More liturgical regulations and prescriptions will never bring deepening faith to our eucharistic assemblies; only love for one another will, and the healing we so desperately need.

Alas, even all these efforts can only be meager strivings. In the end it is God who makes all things new, and we are but sparks of God's creation who seek to live in harmony with the Spirit set free by Jesus who is Lord.

How is the community in which you live being made new, even beyond deliberate human efforts?

Are you "closer to fine" these days? How has that come about?

COMPANIONS THROUGH PAIN

Then they came to Capernaum, and on the sabbath [Jesus] entered the synagogue and taught. The people were astonished at his teaching, for he taught them as one having authority and not as the scribes. In their synagogue was a man with an unclean spirit; he cried out, "What have you to do with us, Jesus of Nazareth? Have you come to destroy us? I know who you are—the Holy One of God!" Jesus rebuked him and said, "Quiet! Come out of him!" The unclean spirit convulsed him and with a loud cry came out of him. All were amazed and asked one another, "What is this? A new teaching with authority. He commands even the unclean spirits and they obey him." His fame spread everywhere throughout the whole region of Galilee.

Mark 1:21–28

*A*t the ticket counter of General Mitchell Airport a young man stood in line in front of me wearing a T-shirt that read "Pain is weakness leaving the body." It came from the U.S. Marines book of wisdom, according to the shirt, and from the cut of the one wearing it he had bought into that wisdom. The implication is that if you feel the pain, you'll know you're getting stronger.

The only problem with that philosophy is that not all pain is physical. Sometimes it's emotional or psychic or relational. Sometimes it feels like a broken heart or a fractured ego or shattered dreams or life without hope. Sometimes it comes in the form of injustice or racism or poverty. At such times pain is not weakness leaving the body. Then it seems more like pain digging in for the long haul, and enduring it seldom feels like growing in strength. Most of the time human pain seems to be some sort of evil settling in, and just as frequently we feel helpless to do anything about that evil, though the Marines would like you to think differently.

We're inclined to say these days that there is a crisis of authority in the air, that nobody listens the way they once did, and that that is why there's so much evil in human life, so much violence and drugs and sex. If people just listened to authority, the thinking goes, life would be better.

So what happens is that more and more folk make more and more proclamations about how "those others" should be living. Warnings against drugs and sex and alcohol say it, yet little seems to change. Protesters against abortion say it, yet little seems to change. Voices opposed to capital punishment say it, yet little seems to change. Rome says it as well, yet little seems to change. So many simply conclude that no one listens to authority any more, as if they ever did with much attentiveness.

The people in our passage from Mark ascribed authority to Jesus. They did so not because he said very much about evil but because of what he did: he freed them from the evil spirit that had set up a home in some person's heart. In other words, telling people to change their lives and how to live and what to do or not do seldom seems to bring about much difference. What does make a difference is entering into their lives and living their lives with them and making the journey by their side. Many of us may find this prospect unappealing, but Jesus did it compassionately and insistently. And that is why Jesus had authority and why the scribes did not—then and now.

Life is filled with people who know how to do just that, and we grant them authority because they cast out the spirits of evil from human hearts. Some are well known, like Sister Helen Prejean, willing to journey alongside dead men walking; or Nelson Mandela, willing to live in one sort of prison because brothers and sisters were living in another kind; or Teresa of Calcutta, who died loving the dying.

Others are less well known, even unknown. Barely noticeable yet indispensable, they are like fine spices making the banquet of life palatable. Without them there is no meal to gather around, only the gruel of survival. They are parents who do not give up on their children, teachers who nurture what no one else is even able to recognize, and healthcare workers who bring compassion and tenderness to the sick. They are volunteers who smooth the way for larger tasks, judges who minister the law with deep care, and managers of business who pay just wages. They are big brothers and big sisters, foster parents, scout leaders, those who visit jails, and countless, countless others.

If pain is weakness leaving the body, then those who absorb it are the disciples of Jesus.

Who has given you authority in their lives? Why? What is the nature and style of your relationship?

Whose pain are you currently absorbing?

TRAVEL LIGHT WHERE YOU ARE SENT

[Jesus] summoned the Twelve and began to send them out two by two and gave them authority over unclean spirits. He instructed them to take nothing for the journey but a walking stick—no food, no sack, no money in their belts. They were, however, to wear sandals but not a second tunic. He said to them, "Wherever you enter a house, stay there until you leave from there. Whatever place does not welcome you or listen to you, leave there and shake the dust off your feet in testimony against them." So they went off and preached repentance. They drove out many demons, and they anointed with oil many who were sick and cured them.

Mark 6:7–13

*O*f all the months in any kid's calendar July is unique. From the first day to the last and all the sun-soaked hours in between, July is vacation time. It is red, white, and blue bunting and lemonade stands and swimming in the local quarry. It is running barefoot through the sprinkler and catching fireflies in canning jars late into the evening because it's too hot to sleep and there's nowhere to go in the morning. And July is camping—in your own back yard or in the nation's back yard—whether you're a kid or an adult.

So every July four of us go camping. Mostly we explore Wisconsin's backwoods and rivers or settle on a Northwoods flowage. We canoe the tumbling river rapids, do a lazy paddle on the lakes, camp on islands or wild shorelines, fish, and lie in the sun and read novels. It's what God made July for.

On one such wilderness river trip, Mike came with a library of leisurely reading, only we didn't discover his suitcase full of thirty-four books until the first night out, fifteen miles down the river. He couldn't understand why we would be aghast and sheepishly explained how he came prepared for any reading mood: some serious theology, a couple of novels (two Michener and one Hassler), some to improve his golf game, others to improve his parish ministry skills, and still others of political and social commentary. Too late, the three of us tried explaining to him how much easier portaging a canoe and gear would be without the addition of a suitcase of thirty-four books. Given our geographical location, the best and only agreement we could come to was that henceforth every canoe trip would begin with a four-man luggage check. Traveling light does make a difference, and now Mike proudly announces that he limits himself to five books per trip. The rest of us give thanks to God.

The Gospel tells of our call to be disciples of the Lord Jesus, of being sent out, and of the value of traveling light. In the midst of July, however, none of us wants to go anywhere but on vacation. The Gospel and our lives don't always mesh, not by season and not by circumstance. Though willing to go lightly with only a swimming suit and sandals, during July most of us would rather not be sent to any sort of purposeful task. No heavy lifting, please; just the beach.

The truth is, however, that all of us are being sent—though seldom, if ever, to another part of the country or to some other nation, and often not even to one more burdensome task. Most of the time we're being sent back to wherever we've been sent for the past ten or twenty years, back into a marriage or back into parenting, back into being a priest or religious or neighbor or worker who must somehow continue caring about one's job and the people who work that job. And most of us have learned over the years that the lighter we travel back in, the easier it'll be, or we keep learning it over and over and over again until we get it right, which for most of us is later rather than sooner.

Parenting not weighed down by biased expectations for one's children is less burdensome parenting. A marriage not wrapped in too many presumptions comes to love more readily. Professional goals not lugging along the heavy baggage of advancement targets, salary hungers, and self-concept trappings make work less like work. Few of us, however, travel life that lightly.

The truth is that all of us already know that. It's just that we have such a difficult time living it for more than a day. Not to say that we fail at living the gospel, because that *is* where the gospel is lived and where we are sent back—to our marriages and jobs and families and all the other venues of life. It's not that we fail, it's just that it's work—in July or any other month of the year.

We'd like to kick out our consciences and do our own thing. But we can't, not usually anyway. So we go back into where we're living with whatever baggage we're packing, most often with the sense that something or someone has called us and sends us to be there. And we do try to travel light, because a suitcase of thirty-four anythings is a heavy load on any trip in life.

In what ways do you travel life more lightly now than you once did?

What parts of your life are still in need of being lightened?

THE PARALYSIS OF SINFULNESS

When Jesus returned to Capernaum after some days, it became known that he was at home. Many gathered together so that there was no longer room for them, not even around the door, and he preached the word to them. They came bringing to him a paralytic carried by four men. Unable to get near Jesus because of the crowd, they opened up the roof above him. After they had broken through, they let down the mat on which the paralytic was lying. When Jesus saw their faith, he said to the paralytic, "Child, your sins are forgiven." Now some of the scribes were sitting there asking themselves, "Why does this man speak that way? He is blaspheming. Who but God alone can forgive sins?" Jesus immediately knew in his mind what they were thinking to themselves, so he said, "Why are you thinking such things in your hearts? Which is easier, to say to the paralytic, 'Your sins are forgiven,' or to say, 'Rise, pick up your mat and walk?' But that you may know that the Son of Man has authority to forgive sins on earth"—he said to the paralytic, "I say to you, rise, pick up your mat, and go home." He rose, picked up his mat at once, and went away in the sight of everyone. They were all astounded and glorified God, saying, "We have never seen anything like this."

Mark 2:1–12

When you're eight years old, a dark basement can be a den of evil and danger lurking beneath that thin skin of floorboards upon which we live amid warmth and love and security. When you're eight, a simple household chore that takes you down into such a cavern of darkness can be terrifying, even paralyzing. Then basements are the lairs of hidden intruders who lurk there to snatch us into oblivion. Appropriate caution necessitates clear and focused attention as well as taking the stairs two or three at a time on the return trip. Breathing is optional. Many a time I stood at the top of the stairs unable to take the first step down into that sunken pit, despite my mother's protestations that there was no one down there. You could never know for sure. Even mothers could be wrong.

Many forces can paralyze us in life. Fear is but one of them. Sin, too, can have such an effect. There are those for whom cybersex has become such a part of their lives that real relationships are all but impossible. For them the risk of self-revelation and the ensuing vulnerability present too much of a threat. Others create for themselves such a miserly hoard of financial security that they become incapable of true compassion, unable to respond to others' needs. For still others a life of lying generates such endless deception that they themselves can no longer trust anyone. Among some individuals physical or emotional violence dulls and obliterates any sensitivity or compassion. For others a critical and judgmental attitude blinds the ability to recognize God's actions in a world that often serves up opinions and courses of action contrary to their own. A lack of prayerfulness or silence in the lives of some people may lead them to be utterly incapable of reflection or self-honesty for fear of what may be revealed or recognized. Sin can and does draw us into darkness and fear, and in the end paralyzes us much more tragically than any childhood basement monsters. Then true evil does lurk beneath that skin where warmth and security seem so assured.

Recognizing the paralysis and admitting it is the beginning of freedom and healing, but only the beginning. At that point recognition and admission are a kind of confession, if to no one else then at least to ourselves, and so also in that silence to our God. Yet in its grasp we can still find ourselves helpless, incapable of risking the steps that take us down into the basement of our lives.

Max Oliva is a Jesuit priest who writes about the "freedom prayer" (*Free to Pray Free to Love: Growing in Prayer and Compassion,* Ave Maria Press, Notre Dame, Indiana, 1994). As he describes it, freedom prayer is an open and frank admission to God of our helplessness, of our inability to save ourselves from the evil that has paralyzed our spirits. It recognizes that if God does not free us, then we shall be forever imprisoned in our inability to be truly human, truly caring and trusting and honest. At such times we have to ask God to do what we cannot.

Oliva suggests that there are times when we may not even want to be freed, despite knowing in our minds that we are paralyzed. Then the best we can do is ask God with our minds, even if our hearts have not yet been converted from the very desire to stay in our sin. But if we ask God to do what we cannot, then God can begin the process of freeing us—from our greed or anger or sensuality or inability to trust or insistence on controlling our own lives or whatever it may be over which we no longer have control.

Then before long we begin to realize that something new is springing up in our lives. Then we are freed both from whatever is paralyzing us and from our own sinfulness, for at that point in our lives they have become so intertwined that we feel incapable of sorting one from the other. At that point the Gospel story has become our story. Like the paralyzed man who is brought to Jesus by four friends, we find that the forces of life have indeed brought us to the one who heals when we were incapable of bringing ourselves. Lowered into God's presence, we are healed of both our sin and what paralyzes our lives. Then we are made new and are able to walk out on our own in the sight of everyone. Then we realize "we have never seen anything like this" (Mark 2:12), and we glorify God.

Is there an aspect of your life that is currently both sinful and paralyzing?

Do you really want to be healed?

THE SPIRIT SIGHS OVER OUR SINS

[Brothers and sisters,] live by the Spirit and you will certainly not gratify the desire of the flesh. For the flesh has desires against the Spirit, and the Spirit against the flesh; these are opposed to each other, so that you may not do what you want. But if you are guided by the Spirit, you are not under the law. Now the works of the flesh are obvious: immorality, impurity, licentiousness, idolatry, sorcery, hatreds, rivalry, jealousy, outbursts of fury, acts of selfishness, dissensions, factions, occasions of envy, drinking bouts, orgies, and the like. I warn you, as I warned you before, that those who do such things will not inherit the kingdom of God. In contrast, the fruit of the Spirit is love, joy, peace, patience, kindness, generosity, faithfulness, gentleness, self-control. Against such there is no law. Now those who belong to Christ [Jesus] have crucified their flesh with its passions and desires. If we live in the Spirit, let us also follow the Spirit.

Galatians 5:16–25

*T*here is something about sighing, especially when it is deep and silent, as if worlds have just been exchanged. A sigh allows us to sit for a moment or two without breathing—just being at peace and without whatever it is we just exhaled, without our worry or our confusion or even our inner pain. A sigh could almost be a prayer for a new spirit.

Hiccups? Well, they're different from a sigh but sort of the same, too. They're breaths with potholes and speed bumps, like gulps of roughage to keep the good air flowing—or maybe they're gulps of spirit to keep the body in balance when it's quite content to stay out of balance, a kind of forced prayer. Then again, maybe hiccups are about something else.

Last week our parish staff went out for lunch together, and somehow the conversation turned to hiccups and their remedies: breathing into a paper bag, a spoonful of sugar water, holding your breath, drinking water from the far side of the glass. We'd tried all of them. Our waiter added one more from the bartender: biting a piece of fresh lemon sprinkled with bitters. He assured us that it had never failed.

We pay more attention to hiccups. Sighing comes easily. It settles us and heals. Hiccups disrupt. There's probably something good, though, about both of them.

The Spirit is like that for us and for the Church, which is to say it's also a kind of breathing. Sometimes the Spirit is a sigh, deep and silent, like when we've been loosed from our sin; and sometimes the Spirit is like the hiccups, drawing attention to ourselves, making sure we know we're bound to our sin lest we be content to stay out of balance. They're both good things, though the loosing is much more comforting than the binding.

For a long time, at least as long as my time remembers, I've heard the Church talk about how the Spirit's power to loose and bind was given to priests, as in "If you're sorry, you'll be given absolution, but if you're not, you won't." Even as a kid that sounded strange to me—as if there might be something God would not want forgiven, at least not until . . . whatever. It just never sounded very godly—to hold on to sin. It seemed almost like God getting even with us for what we did, or like my brother and me measuring which piece of cake was bigger.

Then biblical scholars began to talk about the loosing and the binding as opposites—if you can loose and you can bind, then you can do everything in between, too, so you've got all the power. But I never needed the Spirit to give me all the power; I just needed power enough to put my guilt to rest, my scruples back in the jar, and my fears to a long winter's nap. If the Spirit could do that much to my sin, that was enough.

These days I've been thinking about sighing and hiccupping. Maybe it's because I've grown older and sigh more often. Now when I sigh I find myself deciding to live with life the way it is and saying to myself that it's got to be okay, because like it or not it's all I've got—sin and all. It's not that I think my life is so good or that I'm so content, but I've begun to realize that after fighting with some of my sins for sixty-some years without much ever seeming to change, maybe I just need to let God do whatever God is going to do with it. And so the Spirit sighs, which is another way of saying, "Jesus is Lord."

On the other hand, after sixty-plus years of living I also keep discovering new sinfulness in my life. Not new brands of sin, but corners of life that I've allowed to get dusty by staying out of them. Like greed that I had labeled "being practical." Like protecting myself from being used, which turns out to be no more than selfishness. Stuff like that.

And every once in a while, in a moment of honesty, I'll come across one of those dusty corners, and then it's like trying to swallow a peanut butter sandwich without any milk. It's hard to get down, and then you start to hiccup.

If you had the choice between sighing and hiccups, between being loosed from sin and recognizing hidden sin in your life, which would be more life-giving for you?

PRAYER ON THE MOUNTAINTOP

Jesus took Peter, James, and John and led them up a high mountain apart by themselves. And he was transfigured before them, and his clothes became dazzling white, such as no fuller on earth could bleach them. Then Elijah appeared to them along with Moses, and they were conversing with Jesus. Then Peter said to Jesus in reply, "Rabbi, it is good that we are here! Let us make three tents: one for you, one for Moses, and one for Elijah." He hardly knew what to say, they were so terrified. Then a cloud came, casting a shadow over them; then from the cloud came a voice, "This is my beloved Son. Listen to him." Suddenly, looking around, they no longer saw anyone but Jesus alone with them.

As they were coming down from the mountain, he charged them not to relate what they had seen to anyone, except when the Son of Man had risen from the dead. So they kept the matter to themselves, questioning what rising from the dead meant.

Mark 9:2–10

*P*rayer is a very personal thing for most of us. Some say that prayer is talking to God, but I think that prayer is also part of what happens on the mountaintop, where even the sun grows dazzled and all that is tattered turns light and regal. It's a transfiguration within a moment's cloud of Godly wonder and awe, and it happens to most of us at least once or twice or thrice in our lives. Then it echoes and spirals forever like hoops of God settling about our shoulders. And every once in a while we glimpse our way back. I think that's what prayer is—glimpsing our way back to the time on the mountaintop.

Love is found on mountaintops, or stumbled upon, or fallen into, or flown like a kite, catching the passion that swirls about the summit. It is lived there with all its jagged peaks and crevices, but also with all the sunrises and sunsets our passion can bear. Yes, the mountaintop is passionate love, and it's prayer.

All the colors of autumn are on the mountaintop, browns dappled with orange pumpkins and drizzled with new red apples and burnished gold. It's springtime on the mountaintop as well, borne on the scent of new life: trees yawning with buds as they nudge themselves out of hibernation. And it's summer, too, delightfully lazy and listless, and winter if you'd like—crunching and crackling with crisp light. Yes, the mountaintop is the best of every season cascading right into your lap, and it's prayer.

Poetry, too, is written on mountaintops. Not just

rhyming verses, but words that sing all by themselves, words with a universe in their soul and a rhythm that dances to the strutting of your heart. Yes, the mountaintop is poetry, and it's prayer.

It's a game of poker played on the mountaintop between you and God, dealt by somebody named Life in a shaded visor. It's God who tosses in the ante and doubles your every raise until you're broke, then folds to let you win on a single high jack because God was always better at winning lives than winning at poker. Yes, the mountaintop is a jackpot all your own, and it's prayer.

Death finally comes home to roost on the mountaintop and admits it's all been a joke as laughter rolls out of its mouth and down the mountainsides until all the villages in the valleys beneath are spilling over with laughter, because now everyone knows the joke—that death never had any power at all. One big tease. And resurrection simply stands alone at the top and smiles. Yes, the mountaintop is forever, and it's prayer.

Except that you and I and the Lord can't live there forever—at least not yet—and so we make our way down the mountainside and back among the rubble of our lives, down from the poetry and the passion, down from the jackpot casino and the home of the trickster, down into the everyday living where springtime forgets to come and winter is gray slush and autumn is stripped bare. That's where we do most of our living, at the bottom of the mountain; but that rubble is also the foothills of the place where once we met our God and where our minds spun in unimaginable wonder, and where we wished we could build tents to stay forever.

Sometimes the struggle among the rubble is too great and we grow discouraged. Sometimes it is too demanding and we grow distracted. Sometimes it goes on too long and we forget. But then someone always wonders aloud what it means to rise from the dead. Then someone else remembers the mountaintop and tells the story—and that is all that matters, to remember that we were once there and will be there again. And it is prayer.

*Name a mountaintop in your life.
How was it God-with-you? How did it
change your life, if indeed it did?
Different priorities? Greater peace?
Stronger faith? A still point amid life's
swirling storms?*

*Does prayer bring you back to the
mountaintop?*

FOR WHAT SHOULD WE PRAY?

[Jesus] was praying in a certain place, and when he had finished, one of his disciples said to him, "Lord, teach us to pray just as John taught his disciples." He said to them, "When you pray, say:

Father, hallowed be your name,
>your kingdom come.
>Give us each day our daily bread
>and forgive us our sins
>for we ourselves forgive everyone in debt to us,
>and do not subject us to the final test."

And he said to them, "Suppose one of you has a friend to whom he goes at midnight and says, 'Friend, lend me three loaves of bread, for a friend of mine has arrived at my house from a journey and I have nothing to offer him,' and he says in reply from within, 'Do not bother me; the door has already been locked and my children and I are already in bed. I cannot get up to give you anything.' I tell you, if he does not get up to give him the loaves because of their friendship, he will get up to give him whatever he needs because of his persistence.

"And I tell you, ask and you will receive; seek and you will find; knock and the door will be opened to you. For everyone who asks, receives; and the one who seeks, finds; and to the one who knocks, the door will be opened. What father among you would hand his son a snake when he asks for a fish? Or hand him a scorpion when he asks for an egg? If you then, who are wicked, know how to give good gifts to your children, how much more will the Father in heaven give the holy Spirit to those who ask him?"

Luke 11:1–13

*A*while back I knew a young teenager, not much more than thirteen as I remember him, and just cracking out of the shell of his childhood. For months, as he told his story, he had thought about buying an iPod. He had saved and saved and finally bought what his eyes had already owned months before. He brought it home and spent the day eagerly playing the music for which he had so long waited. And he wasn't disappointed.

By day's end, still swimming in his ocean of tunes, he also found himself beginning to dream of what his next saving-quest would bring him. It was at that point, he said, that he realized he didn't want to spend the rest of his life longing for whatever life decided to offer. He decided that it would be better to live with what he had than with what he wanted. It seemed to him that of the two, the former would make him happier.

Such a strange and out-of-character conclusion for a thirteen-year-old, one that belonged to someone twice or three times his age, yet he talked about it as matter-of-factly as if he were deciding which TV program to watch that evening.

So much of our lives is given over to our wantings—instinctively, it seems. Yet sooner or later we come to discover their futility even as we continue to want more. And because we never quite get there, we find ourselves looking to God for help.

Coming to God with all these wants is not so out of character for most of us, however, especially with God telling us to come and even insisting that we come, as we read in Luke's Gospel.

Yet I wonder if praying for something really increases the likelihood of it coming about. Does praying to find a job or sell a house or make a safe journey or find a lost object help to make those things happen? Well, you may say, it doesn't hurt. Yes, but does it help?

That question has generated long and fevered discussion into the wee hours of many a morning. On the one hand, the fruitfulness of such prayer is attested to by various and numerous accounts as well as by the scriptures.

On the other hand, folks have vigorously quoted other scriptures that proclaim that God knows our needs even before we ask and how foolish it is to think that we will win a hearing by the sheer multiplication of words. There are stories as well of the failure of prayer to bring about some good. Not every basketball free-throw preceded by a sign of the cross swishes through the hoop.

Luke's Gospel, however, adds an interesting note. After lengthy encouragement to look to God to hear and answer our prayers, Jesus concludes, "If you then, who are wicked, know how to give good gifts to your children, how much more will the Father in heaven give the holy Spirit to those who ask him?" (Luke 11:13).

Suddenly it becomes a quest for the Holy Spirit. We come looking for health or better finances or good grades or a new job, and the promised response is the Holy Spirit! Furthermore, no mention is made of all these other needs and desires.

It's a fair question, I think, to ask what we get in exchange. Saint Paul in his letter to the Galatians offers a list of what comes with the Spirit. He points to "love, joy, peace, patience, kindness, generosity, faithfulness, gentleness, self-control" (Galatians 5:22–23). In promising the Holy Spirit, Saint Luke's Jesus promises these human qualities as sure-fire fulfillment for the asking. If you and I really hunger for deep joy, or if we yearn to become gentle or kind or generous, Luke's Jesus promises that the Father will grant it. Regarding all the other things—a new house, someone to marry, improved health, or winning the lottery—well, there isn't any mention of those.

So should we pray for those things, too? That's a discussion for the wee hours of the morning.

What sort of expectations do you bring to your prayer? Why do you pray?

At what point in your life did how you pray change? Why?

CLEARING OUT THE TEMPLES
OF OUR LIVES

Since the Passover of the Jews was near, Jesus went up to Jerusalem. He found in the temple area those who sold oxen, sheep, and doves, as well as the money-changers seated there. He made a whip out of cords and drove them all out of the temple area, with the sheep and oxen, and spilled the coins of the money-changers and overturned their tables, and to those who sold doves he said, "Take these out of here, and stop making my Father's house a marketplace." His disciples recalled the words of scripture, "Zeal for your house will consume me." At this the Jews answered and said to him, "What sign can you show us for doing this?" Jesus answered and said to them, "Destroy this temple and in three days I will raise it up." The Jews said, "This temple has been under construction for forty-six years, and you will raise it up in three days?" But he was speaking about the temple of his body. Therefore, when he was raised from the dead, his disciples remembered that he had said this, and they came to believe the scripture and the word Jesus had spoken.

John 2:13–22

*N*ostalgia drapes itself over the memories of our lives. It lingers like winter in the month of March, even as early spring rains prod the days into a fresher season. It stirs the sap in our veins, serving up strange concoctions of yesterday's grace mingled with tomorrow's promises.

The days that we once lived seem from today's new distance to have had so much more clarity. They seem to have been simpler, purer, more how life should be. But those days are now gone, with or without our consent.

Most of us wish we could do to the temple of our lives what Jesus did to the Temple of Israel's faith life—cast out what doesn't belong, the stuff that shouldn't be there but by some quirk of fate remains. It isn't just the clutter and the busyness that we'd like to clear away, but the very stuff that keeps us from being who and what we're meant to be. It is too much about us.

Parents bemoan all that gets in the way of family being family: sports practices and telephones and business trips and nighttime meetings and children's friends and an entire cache of whatever besides. Why, a family can't even eat together anymore, they say.

Priests, too, lament the encroaching demands of budgets and personnel issues and building needs and rounds of meetings—all that keeps them from the sort of ministry for which they became priests in the first place, they say.

We could be holy, we say, if only Jesus would come and do to the temple of our faith what he did to the Temple of Israel's faith—cast out what doesn't belong—because we don't seem to be able to do it for ourselves.

We try to pray and find ourselves daydreaming about what to make for supper, about the latest family argument, about the meeting later, about how we're going to spend our money.

We try to simplify our lives but we also like our lives the way they are. We like the cut of our style, the thickness of our lawn, the escape of vacation, the high from shopping or chocolate or daytime soaps or whatever flirts with our fancy.

We wish we could love better, care better, have more compassion or patience, be more generous, but original sin always gets in the way; only we don't call it original sin. We say we don't have the willpower or the energy. It doesn't much matter what we call it, though. It's all the same thing. It's all the stuff that's lured our lives away from being what they were meant to be, even stolen our lives and turned them into marketplaces.

So what are we to do? John's Gospel says (even promises) that God will come and drive such stuff from our lives. In fact, the promise is that God will do it whether we wish it or not, which is probably a good move on God's part because most of us are a bit fearful of what God may clear away. So as much as we may want the temples of our lives cleared, the fact is that we also like much of what takes up our lives; and that's why we tend not to ask, because we're not quite sure what God will clear away.

Still, God does come and does clear our temples. The practicalities of life do seem to diminish our passions, much as failure does to our dreams. Whether we are young or old, boredom dulls the glaze of novelty on our toys so that they lie forgotten in the dust. One day we graduate from high school and the next year's football hero or valedictorian steps on to the stage and steals away the remnants of our glory. Our children grow up, new friends lure their affections, and hollows of silence settle on our rooms. Friendships melt into memories with little to keep us busy except for the reshuffling of images. Is it life that clears the temples of our lives, or is it God—or is there no difference?

What is the clutter in your life? What is your life's essence that you wish you could live more clearly?

What clutter has God thus far cleared from your life?

WHAT MAKES YOUR LIFE WHOLE (AND HOLY)?

Do not be deceived, my beloved brothers [and sisters]: all good giving and every perfect gift is from above, coming down from the Father of lights, with whom there is no alteration or shadow caused by change. He willed to give us birth by the word of truth that we may be a kind of firstfruits of his creatures.

Know this, my dear brothers [and sisters]: everyone should be quick to hear, slow to speak, slow to wrath, for the wrath of a man does not accomplish the righteousness of God. Therefore, put away all filth and evil excess and humbly welcome the word that has been planted in you and is able to save your souls.

Be doers of the word and not hearers only, deluding yourselves. For if anyone is a hearer of the word and not a doer, he is like a man who looks at his own face in a mirror. He sees himself, then goes off and promptly forgets what he looked like. But the one who peers into the perfect law of freedom and perseveres, and is not a hearer who forgets but a doer who acts, such a one shall be blessed in what he does.

If anyone thinks he is religious and does not bridle his tongue but deceives his heart, his religion is vain. Religion that is pure and undefiled before God and the Father is this: to care for orphans and widows in their affliction and to keep oneself unstained by the world.

James 1:16–27

*S*ometimes I sit in my chair and think that I should be about better things than I am, though I would be hard pressed to say what those better things might be. Nor would I want to suggest that what I am about is not of value, for it is almost always about others' lives, about their tears and their coming to wisdom and the journeys of their hearts. They are worthwhile moments, I think, so when I stop to consider the nature of such musings, I wonder why I think that there are better things to do. I suspect that many of us reflect on the alternate paths we might have taken.

When I stop to think about the people who have become whole in the course of their lives, I find myself naming folks who have pretty much come to their last days, to the "heel of the loaf," one might say. The other "slices" of their life have fed them and others as well, enough to sustain them through the tears and nourish them in their feasting. Now little remains for them except the remembering.

Curious, too, that I would think of these lives as whole only after so much is used up and gone. A mystery, that the wholeness should arise only in the emptiness, and yet their wholeness seems so much more than mine might ever be.

I think of my grandfather August, who died at the age of eighty after years of working in the lumberyard at Panzer Lumber Company in Sheboygan. I'm not even sure why I think of him as whole, but I do—even though at the end of his life he didn't seem to have a lot to show for it all, only that he was at peace and pretty much lived life as it came along, even the dying part. Yet in the end his life seemed fairly worn and frayed. He navigated his corner of the world with a shuffle. He insisted on cooking his own meals even though they came mostly from cans; and to my recollection he never bothered owning a phone because there was always a neighbor around who did, he said. I'm not sure why any of that makes his life seem whole to me, but it does.

I think of others, too, women and men who at some point in their lives seemed to have it all together. No regrets, they would say, even while admitting that there were parts of their living that were less than exemplary. Still, for them it had all become one in some satisfying and worthwhile way.

Erik Erikson, the psychologist who contributed much to our understanding of the process of human growth into adulthood and maturity, noted that each stage of life has its own task, and that the task of the final stage is integration. I suppose this is another way of saying that the challenge is to put all the pieces together in a way that makes sense. In some ways it's like putting together a jigsaw puzzle, if we stay at it long enough; and in other ways it's like arranging a room full of furniture. There's more than one way to make it all welcoming, but it can also be arranged in such a way that no one wants to live there or even go in.

Jesus pointed out that it's what comes out of our lives that defiles us, things like theft and murder and adultery and greed and an entire catalog of other such behaviors (see Mark 7:21–23). He also pointed out that by implication what comes out of our lives can make us holy as well. The Letter of James says that being "doers of the word" is what makes us holy. It's caring "for orphans and widows in their affliction" and keeping "oneself unstained by the world." In other words, when we arrange the furniture of our lives, goodness makes a better lamp than selfishness or indifference.

What is or has been the primary labor of your life? Do you find this to be the same as or different from what has come out of your life?

What are you proud of? How does this square with what Jesus was about?

LIVING WITH TENSION

Peter approaching [Jesus] asked him, "Lord, if my brother sins against me, how often must I forgive him? As many as seven times?" Jesus answered, "I say to you, not seven times but seventy-seven times. That is why the kingdom of heaven may be likened to a king who decided to settle accounts with his servants. When he began the accounting, a debtor was brought before him who owed him a huge amount. Since he had no way of paying it back, his master ordered him to be sold, along with his wife, his children, and all his property, in payment of the debt. At that, the servant fell down, did him homage, and said, 'Be patient with me, and I will pay you back in full.' Moved with compassion the master of that servant let him go and forgave him the loan. When that servant had left, he found one of his fellow servants who owed him a much smaller amount. He seized him and started to choke him, demanding, 'Pay back what you owe.' Falling to his knees, his fellow servant begged him, 'Be patient with me, and I will pay you back.' But he refused. Instead, he had him put in prison until he paid back the debt. Now when his fellow servants saw what had happened, they were deeply disturbed, and went to their master and reported the whole affair. His master summoned him and said to him, 'You wicked servant! I forgave you your entire debt because you begged me to. Should you not have had pity on your fellow servant, as I had pity on you?' Then in anger his master handed him over to the torturers until he should pay back the whole debt. So will my heavenly Father do to you, unless each of you forgives [your] brother from [your] heart."

Matthew 18:21–35

*S*tress" is a four letter word, one to which someone has added a couple of *s*'s. It's a word that makes us cringe. Despite the fact that we run from stress, it seems to pursue us doggedly. Like a new puppy, it noses its way into our business whenever we move to a new home or change jobs or add to our family or experience the death of a relationship. Combine three or four such experiences at the same time and we can be paralyzed or become physically sick. Tension and stress seem to multiply exponentially.

On the other hand, tension can be a good thing, even a necessary and valuable component of life. Raising a teenager (or being one) can be stressful and laced with tension. The years need boundaries and restrictions but also the loosening of them, and therein lies the tension—when to do which. Ignore the demands of either, and the likelihood of ever seeing maturity begins to evaporate. It's amid the tensions that real life seems to blossom.

Marriage, too, can take some juggling. In one way we remain wedded to who we've always been, and at the same time we find ourselves also married to the personality and lifestyle of another. When to compromise, when to cling to one's own ideals, when to surrender in order to recognize something new being born—it can easily seem like we're ricocheting off the walls of self-identity. Yet out of that tension a real marriage begins to unfold, something we'd never imagined. It's a fruitfulness born of tension.

Examples of such tension in life are countless: the

thrill and the insecurity of moving out on one's own, the excitement and the fear of becoming new parents, the pride and the anxiety of a promotion, holding to treasured ideals and the compromises demanded by life, looming retirement and the opportunities for new ventures. Tension can and does generate fuller life, and it can also be where God happens because God is life.

While the passage from Matthew 18 seems to be about forgiveness and the necessity to respond to the need for forgiveness when the time comes, the parable also proposes a broader perspective. At first reading it seems to be a tale told in answer to Peter's question about how many times one must forgive. Yet the parable does not begin, "That is why *forgiveness* may be likened to a king . . . ." Rather it begins, "That is why the *kingdom of heaven* may be likened to a king . . . ." As with all Gospel parables, this one, too, is about the kingdom of God.

The story begins with a king who is moved to be most generous and cancels a servant's enormous debt. By the end of the parable, however, the king is forced to hold that same servant accountable and cast him into prison. The king finds himself living in the tension between mercy and the justice of accountability, which is where forgiveness is always found—not only forgiveness but just about every other aspect of life—which is to say between the poles of opposites. Like the king, we find ourselves living in the tension of having a foot in each of two worlds. That's how and where we find the kingdom of God.

It's true that hindsight always offers better vision than foresight. How we as a nation responded to the events that have come to be known as 9/11, for instance, how we were propelled into war in Iraq, how we have become ensnared in its violence—all of that would suggest that we might have been better off living with the tension of Saddam Hussein rather than attempting to force some resolution before its time.

The procedures of our penal system suggest the same. While it would be unwise simply to open the door and let everyone free, the finality of capital punishment suffocates every possible breath of conversion. Though admittedly difficult, it would be better to live with the tension of seeking ways of healing and wholeness.

The kingdom of God breaks in upon our world amid the tensions of conflicting poles, maybe because that's always where growth takes place. It's tension that steers us off center and into uncharted waters.

To what new and better place have life's tensions brought you?

From the point of view of an outsider, would the tensions of your life have been a plus or a minus? Why?

PASSIONATE COMMITMENT

[Jesus began speaking in the synagogue, saying]: "Today this scripture passage is fulfilled in your hearing." And all spoke highly of him and were amazed at the gracious words that came from his mouth. They also asked, "Isn't this the son of Joseph?" He said to them, "Surely you will quote me this proverb, 'Physician, cure yourself,' and say, 'Do here in your native place the things that we heard were done in Capernaum.'" And he said, "Amen, I say to you, no prophet is accepted in his own native place. Indeed, I tell you, there were many widows in Israel in the days of Elijah when the sky was closed for three and a half years and a severe famine spread over the entire land. It was to none of these that Elijah was sent, but only to a widow in Zarephath in the land of Sidon. Again, there were many lepers in Israel during the time of Elisha the prophet; yet not one of them was cleansed, but only Naaman the Syrian." When the people in the synagogue heard this, they were all filled with fury. They rose up, drove him out of the town, and led him to the brow of the hill on which their town had been built, to hurl him down headlong. But he passed through the midst of them and went away.

Luke 4:21–30

I sometimes wonder if Jesus ever second-guessed himself. Did he question his decisions or wish he'd kept his mouth shut even when he was right? Or did he simply decide and proceed without a backward glance, like a seedling committed to the sun? Nothing dissuades or distracts it. Is that what happened in the synagogue, that he came to see what needed to be said and so he said it, plainly and without hesitation? And then all hell broke loose, or at least all the Nazareth synagogue.

Henry Ossawa Tanner's painting *The Savior* now hangs in the National Museum of American Art. It is a stark and poignant profile portrait of Jesus, perplexed and perhaps even depressed as he stares at his future's blank and distant wall. It could well be the Jesus presented here in Luke's Gospel passage, wondering how it could have all come crashing down upon him so quickly. One moment the town's most amazing prodigy, the next condemned by acclamation to death by cliff-drop.

If it's true that it takes three positive comments to overcome and balance one negative, what did it take to bring his psyche back from an entire village's rejection? And what kept driving him on?

A friend called during the Christmas holidays. We hadn't talked in months, so it was one of those phone calls that gathers up all the happenings of the recent past, a patchwork quilt to keep the friendship warm.

Early in the conversation, just after we'd said hello and how are you, she asked what my passion was these days.

What was I eager about and driven by? It caught me a bit off guard, only because I had not been thinking about it. As I recall I hemmed and hawed and stuttered something about life in the parish. It didn't seem right to say I didn't know, even if I didn't really. At the moment it just seemed that I should have a passion.

Much later in the conversation she mentioned her daughter's advice to her that she should find a passion—something that would ease the day-to-day strains between the two of them. ("Oh, that's where that question came from," I thought to myself.) "So, I'm thinking of taking a course in photography," she said. "I think I'd like that."

After we'd wished each other a happy new year and hung up to go back to tinkering with our lives, I thought about our conversation, about having a passion, and then wished I'd said that we can't choose a passion because passions choose us, not the other way around. But I hadn't thought of that while I was on the phone, so it never got to be said except to myself, and more than once since then.

Passions drive us and commit us to the count of ten. They don't second-guess. If they are worthwhile, if they come from God, as did those in the life of Jesus, then we stand in quiet courage upon committed lives, as if driven to goodness by some preordained call.

It happens. To Nelson Mandela, imprisoned as if in transparent amber by the unrelenting truth of his convictions. To Rosa Parks, calmly refusing to go not only to the back of the bus but also to the back of life. To a lone and anonymous student remembered forever because he stood in defiance of military might in Tiananmen Square. To the prophet Jeremiah, impelled to be faithful to a Word whose very power reduced his desire to ashes. To Mary, the mother of Jesus, who uttered the craziest of all yesses that set her life spinning out of any control except that of God. To say nothing of teenagers daring to choose uncommon mores among their peers, and heads of households working in jobs without satisfaction in order to support their family, and elderly people reluctantly raising yet a second family of their children's children. Passionate commitments happen. They don't always feel like passion, but they do happen.

It was the apostle Paul who challenged the Corinthian community to remember their gifts and their once-passionate commitment to them. "[F]aith, hope, love remain, these three; but the greatest of these is love" (1 Corinthians 13:13). Commitment does happen. Hence the passion.

To what in your life are you committed for the long term? Can you, would you label that your passion?

What gifts of life have chosen you?

DYING AND NEW LIFE

Now there were some Greeks among those who had come up to worship at the [Passover] feast. They came to Philip, who was from Bethsaida in Galilee, and asked him, "Sir, we would like to see Jesus." Philip went and told Andrew; then Andrew and Philip went and told Jesus. Jesus answered them, "The hour has come for the Son of Man to be glorified. Amen, amen, I say to you, unless a grain of wheat falls to the ground and dies, it remains just a grain of wheat; but if it dies, it produces much fruit. Whoever loves his life loses it, and whoever hates his life in this world will preserve it for eternal life. Whoever serves me must follow me, and where I am, there also will my servant be. The Father will honor whoever serves me.

"I am troubled now. Yet what should I say? 'Father, save me from this hour'? But it was for this purpose that I came to this hour. Father, glorify your name." Then a voice came from heaven, "I have glorified it and will glorify it again." The crowd there heard it and said it was thunder; but others said, "An angel has spoken to him." Jesus answered and said, "This voice did not come for my sake but for yours. Now is the time of judgment on this world; now the ruler of this world will be driven out. And when I am lifted up from the earth, I will draw everyone to myself." He said this indicating the kind of death he would die.

John 12:20–33

*W*ritten on the heart and soul of every created thing is what it is meant to be, and every creature reveals itself to the world. Thus we are able to know rock and fire, water and wind. We come to know the tree and the cloud, the grain of sand as well as the mountain flung against the sky, the hummingbird and the minnow and the giraffe. There is no hiding, none, except for the ones who are human.

What is written on our own hearts, it seems, is masked and muffled, as if waiting to be deciphered. The only way to know what we carry written there and whether it is inscribed by the Lord God or by our own hand is by dying. It is death—the daily dance and the restless lifelong pageant as well as the final act of capitulation—that reveals what is written on our hearts and who we really are. There seems to be no other way to know.

Once I planted a garden of flowers, of color that dribbled and drooled all over the earth and lingered all summer long. The garden just seemed to belong to that summer.

When fall came I decided to gather the seeds, a kind of harvest of leftovers with a promise for the next new season. A handful of every kind I saved, each into its own plain white envelope. I realized that I had no pencil with me to mark what each would become. It was late afternoon and the sun had made me lazy, so I decided not to go looking for some marker and convinced myself that I could remember what each packet held. After all, I said to myself, I watched them grow all summer long. The seeds of the sunflower are broad and bold. Who could not know the sunflower seed? And marigold seeds, they are like shavings wisped from a twig. And the seed of the sweet alyssum seemed like fairy dust. The others, well, they all seemed less notable, but I'd remember, I said to myself. I'd know, come planting time.

Spring came and with it the time for seeding. I remembered the seeds of the sunflower and those of the marigold, but the others blurred beyond the memories of their autumn packing. All I could do was guess, and the flowers that came up that year became a hodgepodge garden of high aster borders overshadowing patches of pansies, miniature carnations lost among tall hollyhocks, and sweet alyssum mixed with zinnias. It was a most strange garden, all because I was unable to read what was written on the hearts of the seeds. The seeds had to do some dying in order for them to reveal what they were. It's much like that with us.

When we humans fall in love, it seems so often we're not quite sure whether it's love or not. After all, maybe it's just infatuation, maybe it's the good times we have together that we love, the laughing and being able to act silly without being self-conscious. Maybe that's what we love, we think to ourselves.

All of that is good healthy wondering, yet we never really know for sure until we experience some dying in the midst of the loving. We don't know for sure if it's love until problems of some sort come along: when there's some serious illness or when we get sick financially or we start seeing some things we don't like in one another or other people start leaning on our relationship big-time—that sort of dying. Then if we can still say "I love you" and mean it without hesitation, that's when we know it's love—when it's not convenient any longer to love. That's when we begin to know what is written on our hearts. It takes some dying.

It's that way, too, with being a person of faith and a disciple of Jesus, and with service of others, and with why we choose the professions we do, and with why we have children. It's that way with just about everything. Why we do what we do becomes known in the midst of some dying.

Maybe that's why we are afraid of dying, because then the secret of who we really are will be out, especially to ourselves. Then what has been written on our hearts all along will be known—no more hiding. Sometimes I wonder whether that's why Jesus seemed troubled, even a little afraid.

What have you learned about yourself from the various sorts of dying you've experienced?

Do you feel closer to God in the good times or in the bad times? Why do you suppose that would be?

SHARED TRUTH

On the evening of that first day of the week, when the doors were locked, where the disciples were, for fear of the Jews, Jesus came and stood in their midst and said to them, "Peace be with you." When he had said this, he showed them his hands and his side. The disciples rejoiced when they saw the Lord. [Jesus] said to them again, "Peace be with you. As the Father has sent me, so I send you." And when he had said this, he breathed on them and said to them, "Receive the holy Spirit. Whose sins you forgive are forgiven them, and whose sins you retain are retained."

Thomas, called Didymus, one of the Twelve, was not with them when Jesus came. So the other disciples said to him, "We have seen the Lord." But he said to them, "Unless I see the mark of the nails in his hands and put my finger into the nailmarks and put my hand into his side, I will not believe." Now a week later his disciples were again inside and Thomas was with them. Jesus came, although the doors were locked, and stood in their midst and said, "Peace be with you." Then he said to Thomas, "Put your finger here and see my hands, and bring your hand and put it into my side, and do not be unbelieving, but believe." Thomas answered and said to him, "My Lord and my God!" Jesus said to him, "Have you come to believe because you have seen me? Blessed are those who have not seen and have believed."

John 20:19–29

*M*ost of us like to think we have a handle on truth, that when we've got something figured out, it's figured out for good. But life keeps unfolding in unexpected directions, much to our constant surprise.

One of Carl Jung's favorite stories was about the water of life. The story is a good metaphor for all of life, in part because it keeps us off balance enough to remind us that none of us controls the truth.

Early in creation the water of life decided it wanted to spring up and be a source of new life for everyone. When it did people began to gather in order to share in its bounty. Before long, however, those who had discovered its gifts began to protect it. They set a fence around it and a guard to watch over it. Someone else put a lock on the gate. Still others began to ration it and to decide who could drink from it and who could not. As a result the water that was life became division and anger for those who had found it. This disturbed the water of life greatly, and the water decided it would cease flowing and find another place to bubble forth, and this is what it did. At first, the people did not notice and simply kept coming to the old place for more of the flowing gift of life. Before long a few of those who had gathered there realized what had taken place and with great courage they set out to find where the new site of the flowing water might be. In time they found it, but eventually what had happened at the first place repeated itself: the water once again ceased flowing and sought out yet another spot. This has been going on throughout all of history.

So it is with what we call truth. It keeps springing up in all sorts of nooks and crannies, at times and in places we'd least expect. And just when we think we have it preserved, it eludes us once more. All of which makes the diversity and plurality of community crucial to discovering its presence.

It's a struggle to accept the fact that there may be some truth and wisdom springing up on the other side of the fence, and even more difficult to consequently admit our need for those on the other side. It isn't only that we balance one another out, but that as a whole we are richer and wiser. Republicans and Democrats, young and old, rappers and classicists.

So in the Church as well—Fr. Richard McBrien and Mother Angelica, those nurtured by the rosary and those who explore New Age spirituality, those who threw out the baby with the bath water and those who still bathe the baby in the same bath water. The fact is that the other side of the fence is us as well, and the fountain of truth springs up on both sides. The Church needs to have room for all of us, conservatives and liberals alike.

- Conservatives provide continuity with the past lest we forget our roots. Liberals are our bridge to a future where truth is experienced from a fresh perspective. Both bear wisdom.
- Conservatives watch over enduring truth. Liberals explore the frontiers of the divine, offering a vision of what can be. Both bear wisdom.
- Conservatives hold us accountable to the truth. Liberals stretch us to deeper truth. Both bear wisdom.

- Conservatives proclaim God to be transcendent, much more than the best of what is human. Liberals proclaim God to be immanent, intrinsic to the human journey and committed to it. Both bear wisdom.
- Conservatives value the mind's need to know. Liberals value the heart's need to be stirred. Both bear wisdom.

Thomas, one of the tradition's great doubters and seekers, was unable to know the risen Lord on his own when he was absent from the gathered community. Only when he was with the assembled believers did he come to recognize his Lord and God. They pulled him back into seeing. Communal living and communal faith do that for us.

So we need one another whether we like it or not, because the fountain of life and truth and all that is God springs up where it will. Alone we are so much less. Like the early community in the Acts of the Apostles, we cannot be the community of faith we are called to be unless we share everything in common with one another, even our truth and our wisdom. Without one another we may not recognize the risen Lord.

What are the truth and wisdom that you need to hear from the other side of the Church? Make your own list.

LOVE IS IN OUR NATURE

[Jesus said to his disciples]: "As the Father loves me, so I also love you. Remain in my love. If you keep my commandments, you will remain in my love, just as I have kept my Father's commandments and remain in his love.

"I have told you this so that my joy may be in you and your joy might be complete. This is my commandment: love one another as I love you. No one has greater love than this, to lay down one's life for one's friends. You are my friends if you do what I command you. I no longer call you slaves, because a slave does not know what his master is doing. I have called you friends, because I have told you everything I have heard from my Father. It was not you who chose me, but I who chose you and appointed you to go and bear fruit that will remain, so that whatever you ask the Father in my name he may give you. This I command you: love one another."

John 15:9–17

Life without love is life without God. Not surprising, when we think about it, for the evangelist John took great pains to point out that God is love. In fact, it's the very power and force of that reality that then commands us to love. No, not as a leader commanding soldiers into battle have we been commanded to love, nor as a parent disciplining a child. Rather, as the yawning night commands the sun to draw a new day into light, or as the unfurling year commands one season to follow upon another, or as light and moist warmth command the seed to sprout and blossom and bear fruit. That's how it is with God's command that we love—an instinct sewn into our being so that we cannot but love. We cannot but be the children of God.

Some will say it is not true. They will point to human greed and indifference and revenge that takes the form of capital punishment and racism and war that turns into genocide. There is no instinct to love, they will say. But what they point to is sin, which is also very real and exists side by side with love in each of us. Yet love is the more powerful.

Bill Johnson is a Methodist clergyman from Appalachia. I listened to him tell the story of how for two months he had been trying to visit a ninety-three-year-old shut-in parishioner who was never home, a curious paradox that made Bill smile as the told the story. Herman lived alone back among the hollows of Virginia without a phone and with only a daughter from a nearby crossroads to look in on him most days.

On one such attempt to visit, Herman's daughter happened to be there and explained that her father was back about a quarter mile into the woods planting trees. Bill said he followed the path back through the woods and into a small clearing where, sure enough, he found Herman planting what turned out to be hickory saplings, about twenty of them. Proud of his newly birthed grove, Herman beamed when he saw his pastor. He pointed out all his labors to Bill and said to him, "You know, fifty years from now people are really going to be happy I planted all these."

How is it that someone cares for those who so far exist only in the mind of God? How is it that someone acts on love when the fruit of such labors will be forever anonymous? Whence do such impulses come if they are not the very daydreams of love, of our God who is love?

They happen all about us, sometimes as "random acts of kindness" casually strewn upon our lives. But in other ways they are also the very stones from which our lives are built, and they come to be the life of the community itself.

Love is Amnesty International crying out for justice and mercy. Love is Bread for the World lobbying lawmakers on behalf of hungry people and Pax Christi building a peaceable world one peace at a time. Love is the Red Cross bearing life; it is national welfare programs sustaining life long enough for it to root (even when such programs are not popular). Love is national health care when the weakest among us lack the strength or the voice to find healing. Love is the Campaign for Human Development offering a future to anyone in need of one. Love is Big Brothers and Big Sisters and the pro-life movement and Call to Action and the United Fund and every such struggle to build a world better than the one we received and upon which others will build even more. Such programs are all imperfect, to be sure, but that's how it is with love.

Such love is much more than random acts of kindness. It is the very stuff of life, love thrusting itself into our comings and goings. It is God gathering to a greatness, like crushed oil oozing through the cracks of our day-to-day living—to borrow an image from "God's Grandeur" by Gerard Manley Hopkins. Or to use another of his images, it is a world charged with God flaming out and bouncing off of all that is, like shining shards of light ricocheting off shaken foil.

List for yourself how the love rooted in your family finds itself overflowing into unexpected corners of life.

What is the relationship between your experience of God and your experience of being loved? Do the rhythms of one follow the rhythms of the other?

CROSSING TO THE OTHER SIDE

On that day, as evening drew on, [Jesus said to his disciples]: "Let us cross to the other side." Leaving the crowd, they took him with them in the boat just as he was. And other boats were with him. A violent squall came up and waves were breaking over the boat, so that it was already filling up. Jesus was in the stern, asleep on a cushion. They woke him and said to him, "Teacher, do you not care that we are perishing?" He woke up, rebuked the wind, and said to the sea, "Quiet! Be still!" The wind ceased and there was great calm. Then he asked them, "Why are you terrified? Do you not yet have faith?" They were filled with great awe and said to one another, "Who then is this whom even wind and sea obey?"

Mark 4:35–41

*Y*esterday's mail brought a booklet from some investment firm encouraging me to plan for retirement. As I flipped through the pages I noticed questions about what sort of lifestyle I would want when I retire, and how I would plan to afford to continue to live the life I'd grown accustomed to. It seemed to be designed to help make the passage from employment to retirement as painless as possible, as if such a transition could be accomplished with little or no change.

We experience reality, however, as a recurring passage from one side of life to another—from childhood through adolescence to adulthood, from being a graduate to a contributor in the work force, from the single life to marriage, or perhaps from marriage into widowhood or divorced living. Sometimes it is inevitable, like growing up or retiring; sometimes it is a choice we make, though not necessarily without fear or anxiety. Still other times we can find ourselves standing on the shore wondering whether or not to float our boat or step into the surf. Crossing over to the other side of anything is seldom as easy as the investment firm's booklet tried to make it seem.

Our Gospel passage from Mark is a metaphor for what is taking place at such moments. Mark says that the invitation to journey to a new and different shore comes from Jesus. He is the one who suggests, "Let us cross to the other side." Thus it is a crossing instigated by the Lord, one that can bring new life. Yet that invitation comes as evening draws on, as so often happens in life. It comes in the shadows of life, where clarity of action is seldom sharp or distinct; or worse, it comes in the darkness of uncertainty and confusion when the opposite shore is not even visible. Then stepping into the boat is undeniably an act of faith. Indeed, at that time in Middle Eastern history, crossing a lake on a dark night without any sort of light to mark home or dock or shoreline might even display a touch of madness, with or without a storm. Who would ever choose to cross at such a time? Yet it was "as evening drew on [that] Jesus said to his disciples: 'Let us cross to the other side.' " And so they went.

It is at this point that they take Jesus into their boat, which is always what is expected of the disciple—that the Lord be invited on the journey, and that the journey to the other side be made together. None of which assures a calm and smooth crossing. On the contrary, the story suggests a stormy experience—darkness, violence, tumultuous tossing, fear, uncertainty, a sense of imminent loss.

The Jesus story ends in calm and stillness, but that is not its promise. What is assured is that faith can bring us to the other side. It is God who knows creation and is in control, it is Jesus who knows the human journey and accompanies us, and it is faith that sustains us in the midst of storms. Whenever we find ourselves moving to a new place in life, we expect the shift to be exciting and welcoming, a fresh beginning. We might even presume that the new destination will always be clear before us and without turmoil, so if the opposite occurs we suspect something went wrong. Yet crossing to the other side of anything is always unsettling. In the end faith is not some spiritual Dramamine® that calms our insides for the duration of the journey. Faith is the strength and wisdom given us by God to ride out the storm. Retirement plans or any other plans do little to assist us in crossing to the other side.

What have you learned from experience about the process of crossing to the other side?

In your life which crossing to the other side has been most difficult? Which has been easiest?

PRACTICING RESURRECTION

Mary set out and traveled to the hill country in haste to a town of Judah, where she entered the house of Zechariah and greeted Elizabeth. When Elizabeth heard Mary's greeting, the infant leaped in her womb, and Elizabeth, filled with the holy Spirit, cried out in a loud voice and said, "Blessed are you among women, and blessed is the fruit of your womb. And how does this happen to me, that the mother of my Lord should come to me? For at the moment the sound of your greeting reached my ears, the infant in my womb leaped for joy. Blessed are you who believed that what was spoken to you by the Lord would be fulfilled."

And Mary said:

"My soul proclaims the greatness of the Lord;
    my spirit rejoices in God my savior.
For he has looked upon his handmaid's
    lowliness;
    behold, from now on will all ages
    call me blessed.
The Mighty One has done great things
    for me,
    and holy is his name.
His mercy is from age to age
    to those who fear him.

He has shown might with his arm,
    dispersed the arrogant of mind and heart.
He has thrown down the rulers from their
    thrones but lifted up the lowly.
The hungry he has filled with good things;
    the rich he has sent away empty.
He has helped Israel his servant,
    remembering his mercy,
according to his promise to our fathers,
    to Abraham and to his descendants
    forever."

Mary remained with her about three months and then returned to her home.

Luke 1:39–56

*H*ow I became the adult I am today from the child I once was I have no idea. The transition is only a faint memory now, like squinting to see through a fog. Then, my mother would tell me much later, I tended to be a perfectionist, ordered, driven to getting 100s on school papers, always obedient, shy, and quiet. How so much of that was left behind with the other fragments of my childhood, I'm not sure, but it was. In high school I learned that being boisterous and a bit obnoxious could bring me friends. And somewhere along the way I realized that one could get by without always doing one's best. While the world preferred perfection, it didn't always demand it. These days I find myself wondering how I grew up without even noticing.

When I think back on it now, I'm not sorry to have left some of that behind. It seems more human this way, not to feel driven to every pinnacle just because it is there. Had I stayed the way I was, had my childhood remained my template for living as an adult, I could easily have dug myself into a pit.

Just as something far beyond my own reckoning unwrapped those bands of would-be death from around my life, so it happens to most of us. We find ourselves brought to new life, sometimes drawn out of our selfishness by a spouse's honesty, sometimes shamed out of intolerance of another by the realization of our own sin, sometimes awakened from our greedy habits by someone's generosity. Sometimes we just grow up. It can happen in a thousand different ways because there are a thousand different voices that call us into life.

Wendell Berry is a farmer and poet who lives in Kentucky. As with Robert Frost, his tasks of farmer and poet nurture one another. The poet side of Wendell Berry wrote "Manifesto: The Mad Farmer Liberation Front," a poem about things to do that don't make much sense, at least not until you stop to think a bit.

He begins the poem by inviting the reader to consider doing something each day that does not compute, as he puts it, and then he goes on to list a number of such activities. Love the Lord and also love the world. Work for nothing. Love someone who does not deserve it. Denounce the government and embrace the flag. Give approval to all one does not understand. Ask questions to which there are no answers. Plant sequoias. Item after item he lists. Berry ends the poem with the suggestion that we "practice resurrection." It sounds bizarre, to "practice resurrection," as if we could raise even a part of our lives out of death. As Wendell Berry says, it does not compute. Yet the entire poem is about finding life where we least expect it.

In the end, however, practicing resurrection is not about raising ourselves but about recognizing that we are being raised to a new way of life, all of us, by some unknown power or presence. The believer would say it is God's doing, so maybe we only need to practice recognizing it when it happens, like being called out of childish ways of life into maturity and adulthood. Then, if we've practiced it often enough, when the time comes to enter into the final resurrection, it won't seem so strange because we'll have recognized that God has been doing it all along. Maybe all we need to do is practice saying yes as Mary once did. Then, as we look around and discover life where we'd never expected it, we'll find ourselves saying with Mary, "My soul proclaims the greatness of the Lord; / my spirit rejoices in God my Savior" (Luke 1:46–47).

How are you different today from what you once were? Are you better or worse?

What are the unexpected sources of new life in your own story?

NEGOTIATING LIFE'S PRICKLIES

[Elijah] went a day's journey into the desert, until he came to a broom tree and sat beneath it. He prayed for death: "This is enough, O Lord! Take my life, for I am no better than my fathers." He lay down and fell asleep under the broom tree, but then an angel touched him and ordered him to get up and eat. He looked and there at his head was a hearth cake and a jug of water. After he ate and drank, he lay down again, but the angel of the Lord came back a second time, touched him, and ordered, "Get up and eat, else the journey will be too long for you!" He got up, ate and drank; then strengthened by that food, he walked forty days and forty nights to the mountain of God, Horeb.

1 Kings 19:4–8

ith a bit of sheepishness I confess that I do not care for "Footprints in the Sand," that piece of pop-poetry about why during the difficult times there is only one set of footprints on life's beach, not because we are walking alone but because the Lord is carrying us. I realize that I am no doubt a shrinking minority in the midst of just about everyone else in the world who deeply loves the poem. I'm not even completely sure why I dislike it so much. I just do.

One summer I watched a father and his four-year-old son walk barefoot along the shore of the lake. It was a warm summer day, and because the sand on the beach was too hot they were walking in the dry stubbly grass paralleling the beach. As they made their way hand in hand, I overheard their conversation.

> Son: Dad, I need to ride on your shoulders because the pricklies hurt my feet.
> Dad: Step between the pricklies and they won't hurt your feet.
> Son: Dad, do the pricklies hurt your feet?
> Dad: Sure they do, that's why I step between the pricklies.
> Son: Dad, it looks like your feet are bleeding.
> Dad: It's just the wet sand.
> Son: I know, but it just looks like your feet are bleeding.

And so the two of them kept on walking side by side.

I think there's a difference between riding high above life's pricklies on someone else's shoulders and negotiating them ourselves. For the believer, the way we negotiate the pricklies (that is to say, life) is not by escape but by faith. Or maybe it's more accurate to say that is how we come to faith— by negotiating the pricklies and not by riding above them. At least that's what Jesus came to say, that God will feed us and sustain us and is there for us but will not free us from the journey, because the journey is the way to faith. Having made the journey, the only possible explanation would be that we have been guided and nurtured by a power so much more than ourselves. And so we have come to faith.

This, in some ways, is the story of Elijah, the prophet of God, who makes a mad dash through the desert to Horeb, the mountain of God. He is fleeing Queen Jezebel, whose four hundred fifty professional prophets he has just embarrassed and exposed as henchmen of the false god Baal, and then had slaughtered. Weary, depressed, and disenchanted by this prophet business into which he has somehow been lured, Elijah is ready to surrender to death-by-desert rather than death at the hands of Jezebel's troops—only to find himself fed by God. It's a good story about how we endure the desert and the journey and the chase and all the rest of life's pricklies. It's also a good story about being fed by more than bread, about being unable to "make it" except by the grace of God.

So Jesus comes to say he is the real bread, the one who really feeds us in a lasting way, because he's the one who shows us how to come to faith and how to live by faith. If we have faith, he says, then we are already well into eternal life, even though it does sometimes seem that our feet are bleeding.

Maybe that is why I don't have a great deal of enthusiasm for "Footprints in the Sand," because it seems to suggest that if we believe, then as a reward God will cope with our lives and we won't have to. Certainly that was not the way of Jesus. He entered into life, was passionately committed to it, was messed up by it, was seldom treated fairly by it, and then was robbed of it, even wondering if his Father were still there with him. And in the end it all collapsed. *That* was when resurrection happened.

Does faith feed you the way you wish it did, the way you need feeding?

On a ten-point continuum between "finding a way to ride above life's struggles" at one end and "walking amid life's struggles" on the other, where do you try to live?

A JUST WAGE

Come now, you rich, weep and wail over your impending miseries. Your wealth has rotted away, your clothes have become moth-eaten, your gold and silver have corroded, and that corrosion will be a testimony against you; it will devour your flesh like a fire. You have stored up treasure for the last days. Behold, the wages you withheld from the workers who harvested your fields are crying aloud, and the cries of the harvesters have reached the ears of the Lord of hosts. You have lived on earth in luxury and pleasure; you have fattened your hearts for the day of slaughter. You have condemned; you have murdered the righteous one; he offers you no resistance.

James 5:1–6

e live in prosperous times, though not everyone shares alike in that prosperity. There are too many who find themselves trying to subsist on minimum-wage incomes, struggle to raise a family without medical insurance, or for whom the benefits of education are tied to race or geography.

Many who prosper are inclined to look upon it as a blessing. Indeed, for them the current prosperity has lifted their standard of living enough to free them from the tension and anxiety of constantly teetering on the narrow edge of economic collapse. This is certainly a grace. Yet for many others prosperity seems to incline them toward greed rather than generosity—a curious and mysterious reversal of expectations. For them prosperity seems to have had an effect similar to the nuclear arms race. Just as there are never enough bombs to provide absolute security, so there are never sufficient monies to guarantee life without collapse.

Efforts to raise the national minimum wage have met continuing and frustrating resistance. Regrettably, even in the Catholic community efforts by laborers to organize and form unions for just wages have been thwarted by those in management and administration, this despite our Catholic tradition that laborers have a right to form unions and strike for higher wages when justice demands a hearing.

Perhaps surprisingly, however, there are a few cities that have enacted their own minimum wage rates, some even going so far as establishing their minimum wage at the federal poverty level for a family of four. In some ways it is not unlike the Gospel story that tells about someone who is not a follower of Jesus casting out demons in his name (Mark 9:38–41). These cities, even though they are not officially inside the realm of religion, seem to have captured the spirit of Jesus' vision. And even though opponents claim such legislation will bring about a loss of jobs due to the consequent lack of sufficient profit, cities that have enacted such ordinances have found those fears to be groundless.

Such efforts for just wages echo the calls for justice from a long line of modern-day pontiffs, most recently from Pope John Paul II in his encyclical *On Human Work*. In it he noted that "the justice of social and economic systems is finally measured by the way in which a person's work is rewarded. . . . A just wage is a concrete measure, and in a sense the key one, of the justice of a system."

For these reasons the hoarding of wealth and the consequent exaggerated economic imbalance cause the words of the Letter of Saint James to grate on our ears like fingernails across a chalkboard. "Come now, you rich, weep and wail over your impending miseries," writes Saint James. "You have stored up treasure for the last days. Behold, the wages you withheld from the workers who harvested your fields are crying aloud, and the cries of the harvesters have reached the ears of the Lord of hosts. You have lived on earth in luxury and pleasure; you have fattened your hearts for the day of slaughter. . . . You have murdered the righteous one . . ."

Which is of greater import, protecting the
unlimited pursuit of happiness/abundance
or narrowing the gap between the rich
and the poor?

Would you be willing to lower your
standard of comfort for the sake of
meeting the basic needs of those who are
lacking?

VALUES TO LIVE BY

Put on, then, as God's chosen ones, holy and beloved, heartfelt compassion, kindness, humility, gentleness, and patience, bearing with one another and forgiving one another, if one has a grievance against another; as the Lord has forgiven you, so must you also do. And over all these put on love, that is, the bond of perfection. And let the peace of Christ control your hearts, the peace into which you were also called in one body. And be thankful. Let the word of Christ dwell in you richly, as in all wisdom you teach and admonish one another, singing psalms, hymns, and spiritual songs with gratitude in your hearts to God. And whatever you do, in word or in deed, do everything in the name of the Lord Jesus, giving thanks to God the Father through him.

Colossians 3:12–17

When Sarah's two preschoolers start going at it with one another, she sits them down at their play table and insists that they stay there until they can smile at each other. It's her way of teaching forgiveness and acceptance; or rather, she says, it's her way of insisting that they learn forgiveness, more from one another or even from their own hearts than from her.

When middle school youth start going at it with one another, more and more schools expect them to use the skills they've learned in something called peer mediation. It's a process much more structured than what Sarah's two preschoolers do, but at heart it's not all that different. It's the process of learning to make one's way into forgiveness, not by grudgingly accepting an imposed truce but by negotiating one's own spirit into healing.

Whether it's the nuclear family or the human family, most folks find themselves striving to live in peace with each other, maybe not always consciously in the image of Jesus, but at least in the image of what their hearts long to be—which is probably the same thing anyway. It's not that any of us regularly do it so well, or even that we always seek to do so. But there is something deep in the human spirit that slowly seems to be evolving into a new sort of human being, though at times through great pain and struggle as well.

The other day I took a brief and very unscientific survey among some young adult parishioners about what they were taught in their growing-up years about living successfully and with satisfaction. Their list came down to such items as making sure to get good grades, living up to their potential, going into business, being nice to people, getting a stable job, enduring hardships, and working for personal achievement. As I listened I could only nod with recognition. I'd heard them all; we all have. They sound so very familiar.

They also sound very different from the values that Saint Paul was holding up to the Colossian community— heartfelt compassion, kindness, humility, gentleness, patience, bearing with one another, forgiveness, love, peace, and thankfulness. While most of us have been taught somewhere along the way how to be compassionate and kind, I'm not sure anyone taught us how to be humble or gentle or patient—just to do it. In fact, one gets the distinct impression that such qualities do not serve one very well in the quest for a life of success and satisfaction. I wonder how many of us would want our children to be humble or gentle or patient in the world of business and professional interaction.

On the one hand we've a long way to go toward the mode of being human that was sown by God in our hearts and incarnated in Jesus. On the other hand, such qualities slowly reveal themselves, whether at the play table of Sarah's preschoolers or in the skills of peer mediation in our schools. It will be a painful process of growth. Simeon promised it to two young parents two thousand years ago in a faraway temple. He warned the new mother then that a sword would pierce her heart and her dreams and her life. Yet ever since, that way of life has been slowly blossoming and bearing fruit, in spite of all the habits that oppose it.

Which quality from St. Paul's list comes easiest for you? Which is most difficult? Which do you yearn for? Which describes you? Which quality describes the ones you love? Which one describes your family collectively?

GROWING INTO FORGIVENESS

Jesus went to the Mount of Olives. But early in the morning he arrived again in the temple area, and all the people started coming to him, and he sat down and taught them. Then the scribes and the Pharisees brought a woman who had been caught in adultery and made her stand in the middle. They said to him, "Teacher, this woman was caught in the very act of committing adultery. Now in the law, Moses commanded us to stone such women. So what do you say?" They said this to test him, so that they could have some charge to bring against him. Jesus bent down and began to write on the ground with his finger. But when they continued asking him, he straightened up and said to them, "Let the one among you who is without sin be the first to throw a stone at her." Again he bent down and wrote on the ground. And in response, they went away one by one, beginning with the elders. So he was left alone with the woman before him. Then Jesus straightened up and said to her, "Woman, where are they? Has no one condemned you?" She replied, "No one, sir." Then Jesus said, "Neither do I condemn you. Go, [and] from now on do not sin any more."

John 8:1–11

*T*here is much about each of us that still needs to be worked out. We are all still becoming—intellectually, emotionally, spiritually—all of us still evolving into the sorts of people God envisions us to be. Even physically we humans continue to be in process.

Our creative sense of sound has developed over centuries. Musical harmony as an addition to melody is a development noted mostly in this millennium, not coming to full blossom in the West until the fifteenth and sixteenth centuries.

Our gift of smell is a sense that continues to be finely tuned as well. We have not yet found one word to describe the smell of innocence given off by a newborn baby's hair, or a word for the charged fragrance of an April day splintered and bruised by a spring thunderstorm. We stammer and stutter, tangled in less-than-perfect words as we struggle to name such an experience.

More recently we hear of growing beyond the five senses and becoming multi-sensory beings, experiencing more than the physical. Our five senses together do help us perceive our physical reality, but slowly generation by generation we are developing an awareness that there is more to life than the simply physical.

We listen to our intuition; we pay attention to our sixth sense; we discover a spiritual side to our personalities. Many people have mystical experiences. They may hesitate to talk about them, but they are so real that those moments give direction to the rest of their lives. It's not about having visions or hearing voices, but it is about the deepest part of oneself experiencing the center of life so profoundly that while words fail, conviction and faith do not.

In *Evil and World Order,* William Irwin Thompson likens us five-sensory humans to flies crawling across the ceiling of the Sistine Chapel who can't see the angels and gods painted large under our feet (New York: Harper and Row, 1976, *Evil and World Order* by William Irwin Thompson, p. 81). Yet every once in a while we "flies" do catch a wink's gleam of the passion that sustains our existence.

Isaiah's God did something new among the Israelites in distant exile, and that same God is bringing us all to something new even today. Yet like Thompson's flies crawling upon the ceiling of the Sistine Chapel, most of the time we are too close to see much of what it is.

More than anyone it was Jesus who showed us most clearly what our God is creating us to be: compassionate and just, generous and merciful, love in a wasteland of indifference. With him the desert bloomed as it never had before.

So when we hear the story of Jesus forgiving the woman caught in adultery and forgiving so unconditionally, of course we squirm. Most of us have not yet evolved to the point of being able to forgive very well, to forgive without any need to equalize the suffering. Maybe that's why we still like the idea of capital punishment and a kind of justice that balances the scales pain for pain. Maybe it's because we are still in the process of becoming human, with such a long way yet to go.

Theologian Sydney Callahan suggests that forgiving is the most difficult thing any of us have to do in life. I suspect that she's right. I am always touched deeply in those moments when I come upon profound forgiveness.

Something stirred in me when John Paul II forgave his would-be assassin. Something in me was movingly caught off-guard when Terry Anderson said of his Beirut kidnappers, "I forgive them. Of course I do. I'm a Christian. I'm a Catholic. I have to forgive them." Something in me was proud to be human when those family members of serial killer Jeffrey Dahmer's victims were able to forgive so publicly and openly what he had done.

Profound forgiveness must still be a new development in human evolution, because I at least am so deeply touched whenever I come upon it. God is indeed doing something new in us humans. St. Paul was so right when he wrote to the Philippians, "It is not that I have already taken hold of it or have already attained perfect maturity, but I continue my pursuit in hope that I may possess it, since I have indeed been taken possession of by Christ [Jesus]. . . . I for my part do not consider myself to have taken possession . . . but [strain] forward to what lies ahead" (Philippians 3:12–13).

On the continuum from justice to mercy, which way do you lean when it comes to capital punishment and the purpose of our penal system?

Have you ever experienced great mercy from someone? Spend some time remembering the moment.

WHO DO YOU SAY THAT YOU ARE?

Jesus and his disciples set out for the villages of Caesarea Philippi. Along the way he asked his disciples, "Who do people say that I am?" They said in reply, "John the Baptist, others Elijah, still others one of the prophets." And he asked them, "But who do you say that I am?" Peter said to him in reply, "You are the Messiah." Then he warned them not to tell anyone about him.

He began to teach them that the Son of Man must suffer greatly and be rejected by the elders, the chief priests, and the scribes, and be killed, and rise after three days. He spoke this openly. Then Peter took him aside and began to rebuke him. At this he turned around and, looking at his disciples, rebuked Peter and said, "Get behind me, Satan. You are thinking not as God does, but as human beings do."

He summoned the crowd with his disciples and said to them, "Whoever wishes to come after me must deny himself, take up his cross, and follow me. For whoever wishes to save his life will lose it, but whoever loses his life for my sake and that of the gospel will save it."

Mark 8:27–35

It's always intriguing to me how we choose to define ourselves, how we explain to someone else who we are. Whenever I interview someone, whether for a job at the parish or for admission into some program, I frequently begin by saying, "Tell me about yourself." Where someone begins, then, is often more revealing than the facts they narrate.

Many choose their family as a starting point, which always seems normal and not so unusual. But some begin at other places—with their jobs, their personal sports history, their hobbies. A while back someone began with a listing of where he went to school, from kindergarten on up to his present employment seminars. He was obviously quite proud of his academic accomplishments, and not without reason, as the unfolding interview revealed. Thus in various ways we proclaim to one another who we are.

Do you remember Father Lawrence Jenko? He was the Catholic priest held hostage in Iran along with journalist Terry Anderson and the other Americans. Some time later, well after his return to this country, Father Jenko told the story of coming to his mother's bedside just before she died. When he walked into the hospital room around noontime, he said, her first weak words to him, and her last as it turned out, were "Did you have lunch yet?" Shortly thereafter she died.

Later on Father Jenko reflected on that moment somewhat wistfully, wishing that his mother's final words had been more contemplative or faith-filled or in some way more memorable. "Did you have lunch yet?" seemed much too unimpressive for the banner one carries in the procession through death's archway.

Yet the more he though about it, he went on to write, the more appropriate those words seemed to be, for that was the way his mother had lived—always attentive to the needs and comfort of someone else. Even her dying breath spoke that way of her life, so much was it a part of her.

All of this would seem little different from Jesus' question, "Who do people say that I am?" and his prediction that "the Son of Man must suffer greatly"—be rejected, then killed, and so rise to eternal life. If someone had said to Jesus, "Tell me about yourself," he would have had no qualms about where to begin his story.

The temptation is always to define ourselves by our successes and accomplishments. Jesus suggests the opposite, that it is more accurate and perhaps more real to define ourselves by what we suffer over, by where we shed our blood, sweat, and tears. The two may be one and the same, because our accomplishments most frequently come about through much struggle. Yet the lack of any "accomplishments" does not mean that we are a nobody. On the contrary, it is when we have not suffered for anyone that we find ourselves wondering who we are. In truth, accomplishments matter little. Who we are is revealed more by where we lay down our lives. That is why believers tell the story of Jesus whenever they gather.

"Tell me about yourself." Where would you begin your story?

Who are you? For whom or what do you suffer? Are they the same or are they different?

Scriptural Index

Page references point to the retreat in which the scripture passage is found.

Topical Index

Page references point to the retreat in which the topic is mentioned.

A – D

F – H

I-P

R-S

T–Z